KNOWLEDGE
Collection

AF887355

Artificial Knowledge & Intelligence

Knowledge Processing

Akhu Sono

to NTVH

ORDER HERE

Consonance Publishing
COSMOS SQUARE INC.
aki@AkhuSono.com

Summary

INTRODUCTION

1. Preface ... 4
2. Content ... 6

SITUATION

3. Key ... 12
4. Roots ... 17
5. Collaboration ... 49

SOLUTION

6. Artificial ... 72

CONSEQUENCE

7. Impacts ... 87
8. Strategy ... 123

REFERENCES

9. Annex ... 129

PROCESSING THE STRUCTURE OF REALITY

© 2023 Consonance Publishing

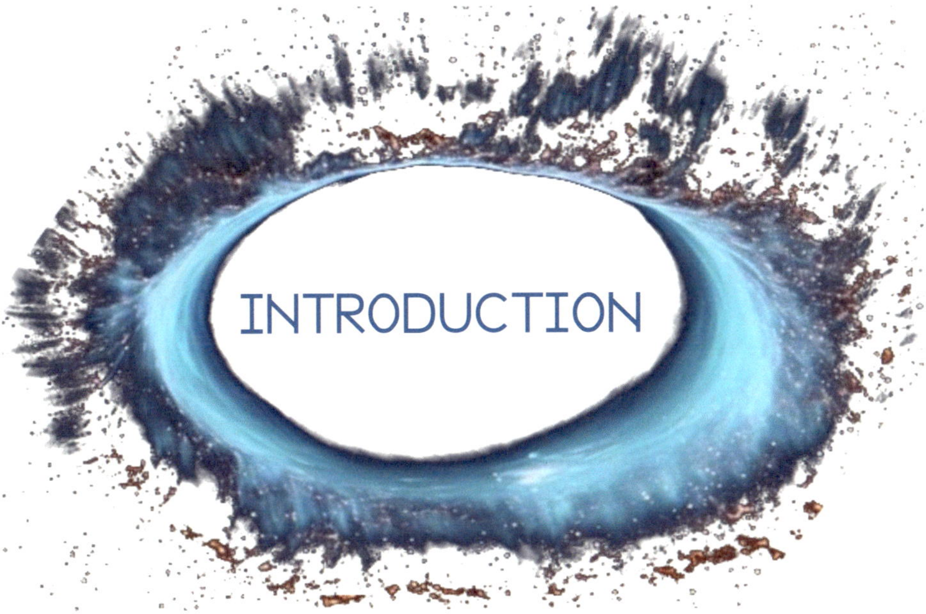

© 2023 Consonance Publishing

1 PREFACE

1. **WHO** : Who this document is intended for
2. **WHAT** : Object, what the document is about
3. **HOW** : Approach, common thread
4. **NOTICE** : Recommendations for the reader

1.1 WHO?

- Technologists and dreamers looking for a sustainable path beyond today's reductive trends may find here some of what could be, as well, as why so.
- Those with a particular interest in computer science, engineering design, or intelligent systems, may also find stimulating ideas & food for thought.
- To learn more about the values and limits of intelligent systems that impact them, everyone should read this document, which proposes a new vision of intelligent systems design and development.

1.2 WHAT?

The term "Artificial Intelligence" combines two terms, where "artificial" refers to computerization giving intelligence to systems, but what exactly is intelligence? What should be computerized?

WHAT IS INTELLIGENCE?

Computerizing intelligence requires a deep understanding of its nature and operation. Clearly defining intelligence, with its scope, purpose and operation is remains a simple starting point.

Everyone uses intelligence. However, typically, definitions of the term are lists of examples of potential cases of signs of possible intelligence, yet with no actual actionable definition that could enable clearly understanding what needs to be computerized.

1.3 HOW?

From a clarified understanding and definition, the document's thread goes back and follows from root causes, as well as the nature and operation of intelligence, to present appropriate design models, and finally considering the impacts of developing effectively intelligent systems, key to a deep knowledge-economy prosperity & solidarity.

© 2023 Consonance Publishing

1.4 Notice

The themes considered are vast, diverse and ramified. Interesting, they support the document subject thread.

The payoff is worth the effort and at least two strategies seem to remain indispensable:

1.4.1 Patience

This approach defines some concepts, in as logical order as possible, because their specific understanding is required for what follows, and builds on these concepts. The reader's patience is key to understanding.

1.4.2 Perseverance

The subject matter is vast and the approach is different. An initial overview can offer a global perspective, highlighting concepts, issues, causes, links, and enabling strategy consideration.

The limits of such an overview, covering such wide territory, remains that no aspect can be thoroughly addressed. Other contexts are required.

Perseverance will be the reader's friend when hoping for more on an aspect, or on many of them.

Some aspects are addressed further in the text, others are addressed in end notes in *section 9.4.3 Notes*. Others still, like those listed in *section 9.1.2 Themes*, are suggested concepts and discussion themes related to the subject and deserve more specific consideration, in different contexts.

The document offers a potentially different perspective, precisely with the hope of sparking further interest and discussion, to which the authors are happy to contribute.

INTELLIGENCE: KNOWLEDGE PROCESSING ABILITY

KNOWLEDGE
BY RICHARD FEYNMAN

https://www.facebook.com/reel/2137429980341533

2 Content

1 Preface … 4
1.1 Who? … 4
1.2 What? … 4
1.3 How? … 4
1.4 Notice … 5
1.4.1 Patience … 5
1.4.2 Perseverance … 5

2 Content … 6

3 Key … 12
3.1 Context … 13
3.2 Meaning … 14
3.3 Analysis … 15

4 Roots … 17

4.1 Nature … 19
4.1.1 Cosmos … 19
4.1.2 Universe … 19
4.1.3 Energy … 20
4.1.4 Reality … 20

4.2 Existence … 21
4.2.1 Unity … 21
4.2.2 Integrity … 22
4.2.3 Causality … 22
4.2.4 Solidarity … 23
4.2.5 Asymmetry … 23
4.2.6 Symmetry … 23

 © 2023 Consonance Publishing

4.3 Transformation....24
4.3.1 Evolution....25
4.3.2 Entropy....26
4.3.3 Time....26
4.3.4 Meaning....27
4.3.4.1 Happiness....28
4.3.4.2 Good....28
4.3.4.3 Beauty....28
4.3.4.4 Ideal....28
4.3.4.5 Prosperity....28

4.4 Knowledge....29
4.4.1 Memory....30
4.4.2 Learning....31
4.4.3 Problem....33
4.4.4 Information....34
4.4.5 Differences....35
4.4.5.1 Hierarchy....35
4.4.5.2 Structure....35
4.4.5.3 Interaction....36
4.4.5.4 Operation....36
4.5 Intelligence....37
4.5.1 Thinking....39
4.5.2 Mind....39
4.5.3 Subconscious....40
4.5.4 Conscious....42
4.5.5 Congruency....43
4.5.5.1 Resolve....44
4.5.5.2 Wake-up....44
4.5.6 Reflex....45
4.5.7 Discipline....47
4.5.8 Feeling....47
4.5.9 Intuition....47
4.5.10 Freedom....47
4.5.11 Science....48

5 Collaboration....49
5.1 Operation....51
5.2 Prerequisite....52
5.2.1 Compatibility....52
5.2.2 Judgment....53
5.2.2.1 Tolerance....53
5.2.2.2 Prioritization....53
5.3 Sharing....54
5.3.1 Process....55
5.3.2 Valuation....57

5.4 Communication... 58
5.4.1 Modeling... 59
5.4.2 Conversion... 60
5.4.2.1 Projection... 61
5.4.2.2 Inference... 62
5.4.3 Integrity... 63

5.5 Security... 64
5.5.1 Authentication... 64
5.5.2 Classification... 65
5.5.3 Context... 66
5.5.4 Entitlement... 67
5.5.5 Access... 67
5.5.6 Cryptography... 68
5.5.7 Poisoning... 68
5.5.8 Monitoring... 69
5.5.8.1 Identification... 69
5.5.8.2 Tracking... 69
5.5.9 Compensation... 70

6 Artificial... 72

6.1 Model... 73
6.1.1 Qualification... 74
6.1.2 Resource... 75

6.2 Archetypes... 76
6.2.1 Entity... 77
6.2.2 Relationship... 78
6.2.3 Processor... 79
6.2.3.1 Background... 79
6.2.3.2 Reflexes... 79
6.2.3.3 Metabolism... 80
6.2.4 Role... 81
6.2.5 Location... 81
6.2.5.1 Position... 81
6.2.5.2 Period... 81
6.2.6 Application... 82
6.2.7 Interface... 82

6.3 Data... 83
6.3.1 Stream... 83
6.3.2 Pipeline... 84
6.3.3 Correlation... 84
6.3.4 Graph... 85

 © 2023 Consonance Publishing

7 Impacts... 87
7.1 Applicative... 87
7.1.1 Existing... 87
7.1.1.1 Qualification... 88
7.1.1.2 Security... 89
7.1.1.3 Governance... 90
7.1.1.4 Integration... 91
7.1.1.4.1 Information... 91
7.1.1.4.2 Knowledge... 92
7.1.1.5 Coherence... 93
7.1.1.6 Ontology... 94
7.1.2 New... 95
7.1.2.1 ML... 96
7.1.2.2 NLP... 97
7.1.2.3 Virtual Reality... 98
7.1.2.4 Navigation... 99
7.1.2.5 Robotics... 100
7.1.2.6 Collaboration... 101
7.1.2.7 Infrastructure... 102
7.2 Collective... 103
7.2.1 Nature... 105
7.2.2 Technology... 105
7.2.3 Social... 106
7.2.3.1 Harmony... 107
7.2.3.2 Quality... 109
7.2.3.3 Education... 110
7.2.3.3.1 Program... 110
7.2.3.3.2 Role... 110
7.2.3.4 Democracy... 111
7.2.3.5 Values... 112
7.2.4 Economy... 113
7.2.4.1 Reduction... 114
7.2.4.2 Transition... 115
7.2.5 Framework... 118
8 Strategy... 123
8.1 Plan... 123
8.2 Prototype... 125
8.3 Standards... 127

9 Annex... 129

9.1 Fabric... 129
9.1.1 Contribution... 130
9.1.1.1 Guidance... 130
9.1.1.2 Revision... 130
9.1.1.3 AI... 130
9.1.1.4 Complement... 130
9.1.1.5 Organization... 130
9.1.2 Themes... 131

9.2 Examples... 132

9.2.1 Nature... 132
9.2.1.1 Ants... 133
9.2.1.2 Crows... 133
9.2.1.3 Bees... 133
9.2.1.4 Spiders... 134
9.2.1.5 Dragonflies... 134
9.2.1.6 Namib Circles... 134
9.2.1.7 Memory... 135
9.2.1.8 Phenomenon... 136
9.2.1.9 Forces... 137
9.2.1.10 Relation... 138

9.2.2 AI... 139
9.2.2.1 Capabilities... 140
9.2.2.2 Intelligence... 141
9.2.2.3 Artificial Intelligence... 142
9.2.2.4 Governments... 143

9.3 Reflections... 144
9.3.1 Vision... 144
9.3.2 Structures... 145
9.3.3 Collaboration... 146
9.3.4 Restructure... 147
9.3.5 Market... 148
9.3.6 Thermodynamics... 149
9.3.7 Collapse... 151
9.3.8 Integrity... 152

9.4 Indices... 153
9.4.1 Glossary... 153
9.4.2 Links... 154
9.4.3 Notes... 157

© 2023 Consonance Publishing

© 2023 Consonance Publishing

3 Key

Trying to contextualize fundamental knowledge & intelligence related concepts, this section presents a rather typical use case that also allows taking a closer look at knowledge, intelligence and information operations.

More specifically, the example considers aspects like:

- Knowledge sharing
- Communication & information
- Relations & differences between Knowledge & Information
- Natural integration of security into knowledge sharing
- How intuitive knowledge processing and sharing are
- Knowledge backgrounds[i]
- Trust

In this example, the sentence "The key is on the table" is the shared information, indicating that a key is on a table.

Yet a brief observation of its natural knowledge sharing context reveals a much deeper process.

Let's successively consider:

1. the context
2. the scope or meaning
3. a brief analysis of some implications

 © 2023 Consonance Publishing

3.1 Context

About to pick up the partner at the airport, one realizes that the car won't start.

This pickup is critical, so one runs to the friend and neighbor next door, working on his yard, and says:

- "Hi, I have to pick up my partner at the airport, but the car won't start."

The busy friend replies:

- "**The key is on the table**."

There is a table right there in the entrance, but there is no key on it. One moves to the kitchen, but there is no key on the table.

Looking around, one can see a set of keys hanging on a hook on the wall, in the corner, one recognizes the neighbor's car key in the set and takes it.

On return, one brings a few good bottles of wine to end the day together, around a good meal, sharing about the wife's trip and things.

© 2023 Consonance Publishing

3.2 Meaning

What is the contextualized meaning of the reply: "The key is on the table" ?

In this context, the effective meaning (the shared knowledge) of the sentence "The key is on the table" in the reply can be summarized as:

- Hi to you my dear neighbor and long-time friend, I appreciate you. Our last dinner together comes back to me ...
- I hope that you, your partner, family, and all are well and that otherwise, everything is fine
- I am currently busy, but I hear your request and will support you however I can
- I know that you are law-abiding and have driver license and valid insurance
- I know that you understand that I am lending you my car for this pickup. I am not giving it to you and that you need to return it intact, right after
- We both know that you are solely responsible for any costs or damages associated with the car, while under your supervision and when driving
- We both know that, since we have an insurance system, a legal system, a police system, and a prison system, if you are not fully responsible, we will sue you and could even get to take the shirt off your back
- When you come back, we can have a drink and a barbecue together, while your partner can tell us about its trip
- Take the car. The key could be on the table or around. My wife is the last ...

Also,

- ✔ There was no key on the table, nor on the kitchen table, but a set of keys was hooked on the wall, with an electronic rod-less car key
- ✔ On return, one took the opportunity to pick-up some wine bottles for the BBQ dinner with everyone, afterwards, and to thank them for their kind support

 © 2023 Consonance Publishing

3.3 Analysis

The "Key" example puts into context a number of determining concepts related to computerizing (making artificial) knowledge and intelligence.

The table below highlights some of these aspects, linking them to elements of the example :

A	Description	"Key"
NATURE	Natural, knowledge is processed and shared intuitively and sub-consciously, mostly.	Naturally, even without exchanging information, friends can share deeply.
CONTEXT	Words, sentences, information, do not count for much as the effective meaning is determined by the specific contexts, starting with the respective parties' knowledge-backgrounds.	There is no key on the table or on any other.
BACKGROUND	More than fine words, the main success factors for knowledge processors[ii], start with: • intention complementarity, at the time • knowledge-background compatibility, in context Information remains a useful communication and formalization tool.	Friends can understand each other deeply, proportionally to the compatibility of their respective knowledge background.
METABOLISM[iii]	Intuitive, mostly subconscious, each processor's metabolism combines internal knowledge-background optimization and evolution processes. Metabolism is a natural priority, essential to survival, development and evolution. See also *section 6.2.3.3 Metabolism*.	Through experience and interaction with the outside world (streams), each knowledge processor evolves its knowledge background.
D	Knowledge & information are very different.	In this case, the shared

A	Description	"Key"
I F F E R E N C E	Understanding the specifics of those differences seems key to their management, as well as critical to computerizing them, their operations and that of every process that uses either.	knowledge was operational and the key was found, despite properly shared false information.
C O M M U N I C A T I O N	Communication is a complex and brittle collaboration tool, further considered in chapter 5 Collaboration. Collaboration uses communication to transfer information artifacts (messages, documents), between alternating senders & receivers. Knowledge uses collaboration which uses communication which uses information, a convention-based encoding tool.	Brittle, communication is especially useful for recording & formalizing collective specifications, as the driver permit or insurance documents. Projection & inference map & convert between knowledge & information.
S E C U R I T Y	Many security aspects, some quite sophisticated, are seamlessly integrated into knowledge and its sharing, as in the example.	The shared information seems almost irrelevant, as the shared knowledge seems much more determining for the activity.
T O L E R A N C E	Knowledge and intelligence are tolerant as tolerance is key to their operation. Everything is relative, nothing is perfect. Tolerance is complex, since it depends on the context, as well as on the qualified relationship of each resource. It is a process of parameterized behavior modulation. Managing qualified relationships remains the key to tolerance management.	Keys on the hook were relatively easily found and the vehicle key identified. It could have been trickier: Which table: in the entrance, the living room, the backyard, the kitchen? ...

© 2023 Consonance Publishing

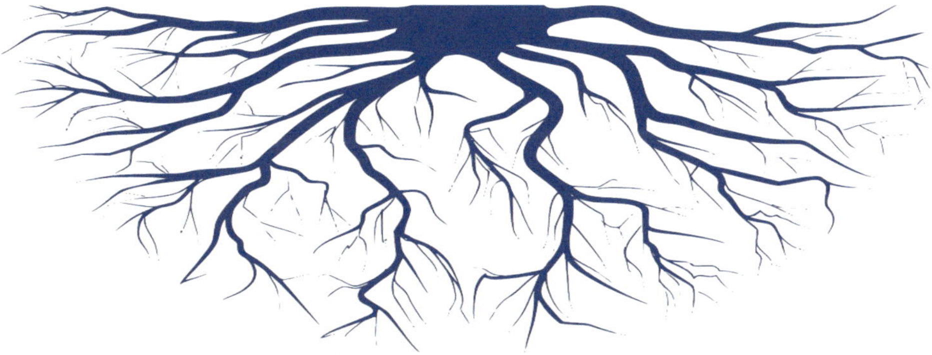

4 Roots

As Albert Einstein noted, problem solving is a direct result of understanding and resolving the root causes involved.

On the other hand, evolving is an intelligent process, based on knowledge of what exists, and the intelligence to improve it.

So what are intelligence and knowledge? What are the roots, nature and operation of these natural, essentially subconscious phenomena, built on each other and on others, right back to the origins of existence?

To computerize (artificialize) knowledge and intelligence requires a precise understanding of the roots to better understand what we are trying to computerize.

An overview of the root causes also provides the context for clarifying the terms and definitions that will help articulate the right solutions.

This section 4 considers the roots of intelligence and knowledge, as well as some definitions (italicized in the text) and concepts essential to understanding and solving them, as to the reading of this document.

Not all potential definitions of a term are included, only those related to the term's usage in the text.

Section 9.4.1 Glossary provides an alphabetical index of defined terms.

Technical" concepts more specific to computerization are introduced in *section 6 Artificial*.

End-notes are numbered sequentially, in Roman numerals, and are attached to the first use of certain terms in the text. Their definitions can be found in *section 9.4.3 Notes*, at the corresponding number.

The section considers concepts that root knowledge and intelligence:

ROOT CAUSES BY LOGICAL LAYER	
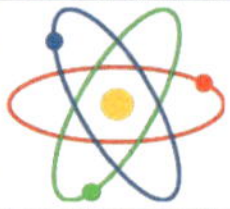	1. **Nature** The Nature of Existence ▪ Cosmos, Universe, Energy, Reality
	2. **Operation** Existence's Operational Principles ▪ Unity, Integrity, Causality ▪ Solidarity, Asymmetry, Symmetry
	3. **Transformation** Existence's Sustained Transformation ▪ Evolution, Entropy ▪ Time, Meaning
	4. **Knowledge** Existence of Knowledge of Existence ▪ Memory, Learning, Problem ▪ Information, Difference
	5. **Intelligence** Intelligence Elements ▪ Thought, Mind ▪ Subconscious, Conscious ▪ Congruence, Reflex ▪ Feeling, Intuition ▪ Freedom, Science

> KNOWLEDGE IS HAVING THE RIGHT ANSWERS
> INTELLIGENCE IS ASKING THE RIGHT QUESTIONS
> WISDOM IS KNOWING WHEN TO ASK THE RIGHT QUESTIONS
>
> RICHARD FEYNMAN

 © 2023 Consonance Publishing

4.1 NATURE

FUNDAMENTAL TERMS AND CONCEPTS ON THE NATURE & FABRIC OF EXISTENCE AND WHAT FLOWS FROM IT	1. COSMOS 2. UNIVERSE 3. ENERGY 4. REALITY

4.1.1 COSMOS

The Cosmos is everything, all that exists (Reality) and all that enables it:

- Universe: All that exists, reality
- Principles: All that enables and supports existence

ALL THAT EXISTS + ALL THAT ENABLES IT

Fundamental principles include those of natural logic, the logic of existence, causality and transformation. Those that also support "common sense" logic.

Some of these principles are more directly relevant to this document's object, and are so introduced starting in the following section 4.2 Existence, beginning with the first or source principle: Oneness.

4.1.2 UNIVERSE

The Universe is *all that exists, structuring energy fields, propagating and transforming between concentration and dissipation.*

For this document, Universe also includes all existing universes, as well as their containers.

"Universe" and "Existence" are almost synonyms, describing the same reality from different viewpoints: the first more physical or material oriented and the second more focused on interaction.

	FIRE BY RICHARD FEYNMAN https://www.facebook.com/reel/1415251816356180

4.1.3 *Energy*

Energy instantiates the Universe.. Toroidal fields of energy (light) waves in a logical, causal universe transforming through Entropy and Evolution. Everything is energy as there is only energy.

PHYSICAL MATTER IS MUSIC SOLIDIFIED

PYTHAGORAS

Intelligent, in forever search of beauty and perfection, subject to Entropy which dissipates it, yet ensures structure diversity and recycling, Energy evolves, concentrates, dissipates and learns through the experience and evolution of its structures and reality. As Energy learns, structures, recycles, and evolves, knowledge is its transforming structure.

See section 9.3.2 Structures, sections 9.2.1.9 Forces, *9.2.1.10 Relation*.

ENERGY INSTANTIATES KNOWLEDGE

	Energy by Richard Feynman https://www.youtube.com/watch?v=2I4VMtDczQE

4.1.4 *Reality*

Reality is the realization of existence and, by extension, of the Cosmos. Reality also commonly refers to the universe and its evolution. See Energy.

REALITY IS THE EVOLUTION OF ENERGY

	Reality by Richard Feynman https://www.facebook.com/reel/1076700164643142

© 2023 Consonance Publishing

4.2 EXISTENCE

TERMS & CONCEPTS RELATED TO PRINCIPLES & PHENOMENA ROOTING EXISTENCE'S OPERATION & TRANSFORMATION

1. UNITY
2. SOLIDARITY
3. ASYMMETRY
4. INTEGRITY
5. CAUSALITY

4.2.1 UNITY

Seemingly paradoxical, Oneness, the root principle, states that:

ALL IS ONE

- **One**: is the transforming energy that is everything
- **All**: is the infinity of energy's forms and evolving structures

The universal principle, on any scale, is that each Element of the Whole has a relative autonomy and independence that enables it to collaborate with other elements of the Whole.

This evolution of the All, in One, is powered by Transformation, through two complementary, yet opposing facets of the Force, powering Transformation:

- **Solidarity**: Unifier, Evolution's engine and structuring principle
- **Asymmetry**: Differentiator, Entropy's engine and de-structuring principle

See also *section 4.3 Transformation*.

ALL IS ENERGY

QUANTUM RELATIVITY
BY RICHARD FEYNMAN

https://www.facebook.com/reel/1912105713003020

4.2.2 Integrity

NOTHING IS LOST, NOTHING IS GAINED, EVERYTHING TRANSFORMS

LAVOISIER

Under causality and transformation, (energy) integrity is maintained.
(1st law of thermodynamics)

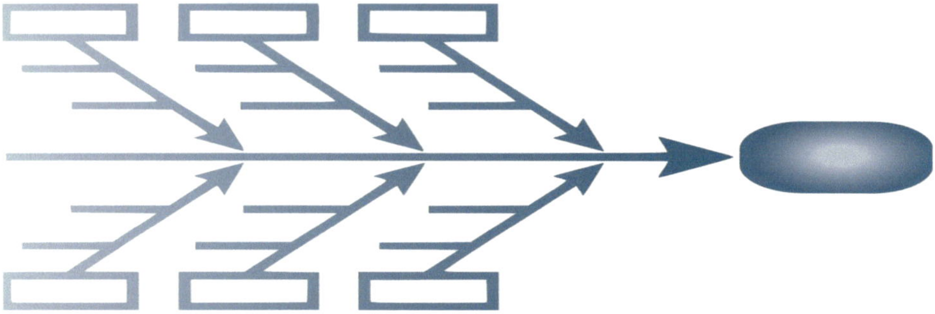

4.2.3 Causality

Causality ensures that causes and consequences are forever intertwined, where each cause has its consequences and each consequence has its causes.

The strict causality that governs reality and existence also frames and shapes natural logic and its application.

Causes and effects cascade into long interdependent chains.

Relativity is a consequence of causality.

STRICT CAUSALITY => ABSOLUTE RELATIVITY

Strict causality imposes absolute relativity. Any other absolute can only be defined as "that which is not relative/causal," which seems absolutely relative.

Everything depends on, and influences everything in its own way. Not only does every cause have its consequences and every consequence have its causes, but every consequence also constitutes a cause of other consequences.

Each entity has its own perceptions and interpretations of the realities it can or cannot influence.

See also *section 4.3 Transformation.*

TO BE SURE, I DOUBT EVERYTHING

DESCARTES

 © 2023 Consonance Publishing

4.2.4 SOLIDARITY

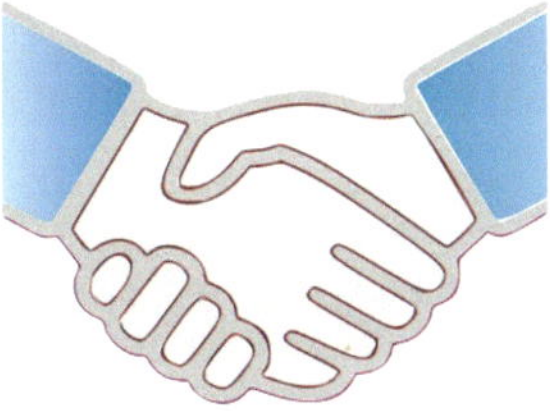

Solidarity is the great unifying force relating everything, aiming for Oneness and providing unity. Solidarity powers Evolution as the great assembler & concentrator of energy.

Fruit & tool of Collaboration, which it also powers, Solidarity operates under various forms, including:

FORCE		COLLABORATORS
GRAVITY	SOLIDARITY OF	Masses
ELECTROMAGNETISM	SOLIDARITY OF	Charges
WEAK FORCES	SOLIDARITY OF	Electrons and core
STRONG FORCES	SOLIDARITY OF	Core particles
QUANTUM ENTANGLEMENT[IV]	SOLIDARITY OF	Quanta
SOLIDARITY	SOLIDARITY OF	Collaborators

LOVE SEEMS TO BE THE MOST EVOLVED FORM OF SOLIDARITY

ENTANGLEMENT BUILDS ON COMMON KNOWLEDGE

	ENTANGLEMENT BY RICHARD FEYNMAN https://www.facebook.com/reel/2029425094270557		**ASYMMETRY** BY RICHARD FEYNMAN https://www.facebook.com/reel/1825114308154813

4.2.5 ASYMMETRY

Asymmetry is the differentiating, dissipating, dividing and recycling principle for obsolete evolved structures.

Opposite and complementary to Solidarity, Asymmetry operates Entropy, dividing and dissipating deprecated structures and their energy.

Dividing asymmetrically, Asymmetry ensures that each resource, at any scale, is unique, that no two are ever identical, in neither nature nor experience.

4.2.6 SYMMETRY

Symmetry is that which is not asymmetrical. Symmetry is part of a universal quest for ideal & perfection, always relative, never complete, guiding choices, thought, structure and evolution, at the very heart of everything.

© 2023 Consonance Publishing

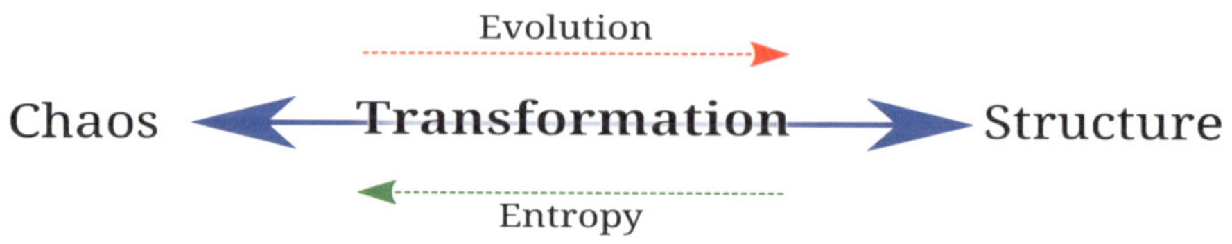

4.3 TRANSFORMATION

In its strictly causal universe, energy is in permanent transformation, on an axis between chaos and structure. Transformation is driven by opposite yet complementary aspects of force, asymmetry and solidarity, affecting energy concentration:

- Evolution develops structure from component collaboration solidarity. Hydrogen is the solidarity from the proton and electron collaboration. Evolution concentrates energy in increasingly sophisticated structures, with greater resolution and contribution capabilities.
- Entropy breaks down structures and dissipates energy towards chaos.

EVERYTHING TRANSFORMS

ANTOINE LAVOISIER

Entropy ensures the recycling necessary for evolution. Evolution is existential for energy, its permanent and ultimate objective.

Everything transforms constantly. Transformation creates and governs :

- **Existence**: the evolution of energy
- **Time**: indexing existence, energy transformation

The most obvious and personal relatable example must be in eating, where living beings "entropize[v]" (digest) others, in order to evolve.

 © 2023 Consonance Publishing

TRANSFORMATION ...	
• *INTERLACES ENTROPY & EVOLUTION* • *CREATES TIME, ITS INDEX* • *FRAMES EXISTENCE OPERATION & PURPOSE*	1. ENTROPY 2. EVOLUTION 3. TIME 4. MEANING

4.3.1 EVOLUTION

Evolution is the existential natural phenomenon that concentrates Energy, by understanding, improving and developing structures.

ALL THAT EXISTS IS FRUIT & TOOL OF EVOLUTION

Evolution learns, understands and improves structures of interest, by building on two main phenomena, intrinsics to Energy:

- Knowledge: the structure of the reality of interest
- Intelligence: understanding, vision, development for improving structures

Opposite to Entropy (see below), Evolution concentrates Energy into new or improved structures, rather than dissipating it. Without Evolution, with only Entropy and randomness, the reality remains in its initial chaos. Yet, so far, Evolution develops an infinitely rich, complex, structured and coherent reality.

Evolution does not just apply to physical structures. In fact, Energy evolves increasingly sophisticated resolvers, capable of resolving ever more complex problems, in order to be able to better concentrate Energy, through contribution to the meaning and purpose of existence.

Evolving begins with an understanding of existing reality, its structure and its operation. This understanding enables improving, or better, replacing the operational structure of the existing reality.

Fruit and tool of Evolution, everything contributes to this evolution. Every existing thing evolves at least throughout its lifetime. Parents die happy, having enabled their children to further contribute to evolution.

WITHOUT EVOLUTION, CHAOS WOULD BE THAT MUCH GREATER

Evolution may not be able to eliminate chaos, but operates as if it worth a try. It may not be wrong. It evolves intelligence and, knowledge, resolving ever more complex problems and better concentrating energy.

EVOLVING
BY RICHARD FEYNMAN

https://www.youtube.com/watch?v=g9qmF6zicPQ

4.3.2 Entropy

Entropy[vi] *is the great structure recycler, dividing structures asymmetrically to better dissipate their energy.*

Driven by asymmetry, or asymmetric division, entropy recycles outdated structures, making their energy available to evolve new structures.

Opposite and complementary to evolution, Entropy breaks-down structures, returning their energy to "chaos". Erosion is an example of an entropic manifestation.

4.3.3 Time

Induced by Transformation and Causality, Time is a Fundamental dimension, of unlimited granularity[vii].

GRANULARITY LEVELS

Time differentiates, measures and indexes Causality, Transformation, as well as evolution and entropy. The many interesting facets of perceptual time are not covered here. Causal Time stretches along reality's existence.

This video presents some of Richard Feynman's instructive views about time:

	Time by Richard Feynman https://www.facebook.com/reel/1298511628812475

© 2023 Consonance Publishing

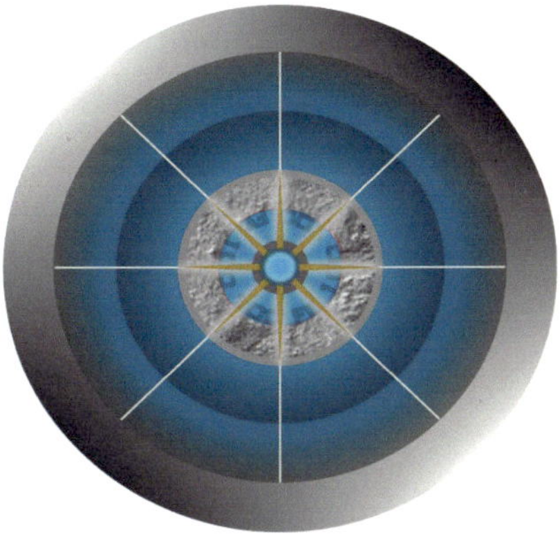

4.3.4 MEANING

For all that exist, as evolution fruits & tools, the meaning of existence is to contribute to evolution to the limits of respective inherited & acquired abilities.

CONTRIBUTE TO EVOLUTION
TO THE LIMITS OF RESPECTIVE ABILITIES

Registered deep at the core of each entity, the meaning of existence is fundamental and constitutes the primary foundation for every value scale or ethics code. In fact, everything derives from the meaning of existence.

DO WHAT YOU CAN, WITH WHAT YOU HAVE, WHERE YOU ARE
THEODORE ROOSEVELT

ISN'T MADNESS TO VIEW
THE WORLD AS IT IS
RATHER THAN AS IT SHOULD BE?
JACQUES BREL

THE MOST IMPORTANT THING IS TO LIVE A MORAL LIFE, TO BE KIND
HONEST, TRUTHFUL, PATIENT, COURAGEOUS, UNSELFISH.
TO LIVE NOT FOR ONESELF, BUT FOR OTHERS.
HELP OTHERS TO MAKE THE WORLD A BETTER PLACE.
LEAVING BEHIND A LIFE THAT HAS BEEN USEFUL
NOT A LIFE THAT HAS BEEN WASTED.
THIS IS THE TRUE MEANING OF LIFE
LEO TOLSTOY

Several phenomena, also fruits and tools of evolution, also operate in the context of the meaning of existence, such as the following natural indicators:

4.3.4.1 Happiness

The Happiness/Unhappiness axis indicates to knowledge processors (human, intelligent systems), the level of its congruence to the meaning of existence.

4.3.4.2 Good

The Good/Bad axis qualifies congruence to the meaning of existence:

- **Good**: *Effectively contributes to evolution*
- **Bad**: *Badly or not contributing to evolution (Devolution)*

> **EVIL IS THE FORCE THAT BELIEVES ITS KNOWLEDGE IS COMPLETE**
>
> DR JORDAN PETERSON

4.3.4.3 Beauty

The Beauty/Ugly axis indicates the structure of reality harmony level, guiding better contribution to evolution.

4.3.4.4 Ideal

The ideal is what we seek, it's what we don't have. In a strictly causal and relative context, the ideal is the integrated absolute, perfection.

The search for symmetry, harmony and beauty are quest for ideals that guide experience and contribution to evolution.

4.3.4.5 Prosperity

Prosperity results from the productivity of collaboration and solidarity.

Prosperity is sustained and equitably distributed wealth.

In principle, in the context here, "equitably" is relative to contribution to collaboration.

> **INSPIRATION EXISTS, BUT IT HAS TO FIND YOU WORKING**
>
> *PABLO PICASSO*

 © 2023 Consonance Publishing

INTRINSIC TO ENERGY, KNOWLEDGE MODELS THE STRUCTURE OF REALITY

1. MEMORY
2. LEARNING
3. PROBLEM
4. INFORMATION
5. DIFFERENCE

4.4 KNOWLEDGE

Fundamental natural phenomenon and intrinsic motor of evolution, knowledge models the structure of reality.

Since its origins, evolution has always adapted to natural phenomena, in infinite ways like, for example, by developing :

- lungs to take advantage of the properties of oxygen
- limbs to better take advantage of terrestrial gravity
- intelligence to process knowledge/structure of reality

Knowledge and intelligence are natural phenomena developed by nature. Knowledge models the structure of reality. Its extension, intelligence, is the ability to process it.

Naturally, knowledge and intelligence are intuitive, precisely because they are built on natural phenomena, whose deep understanding is prerequisite to making them “artificial”.

Knowledge is the foundation of evolution, thought, knowledge, consciousness, learning and action.

Other sections, hereafter, further consider various aspects of knowledge, such as its nature, persistence and relationships with information and communication.

© 2023 Consonance Publishing

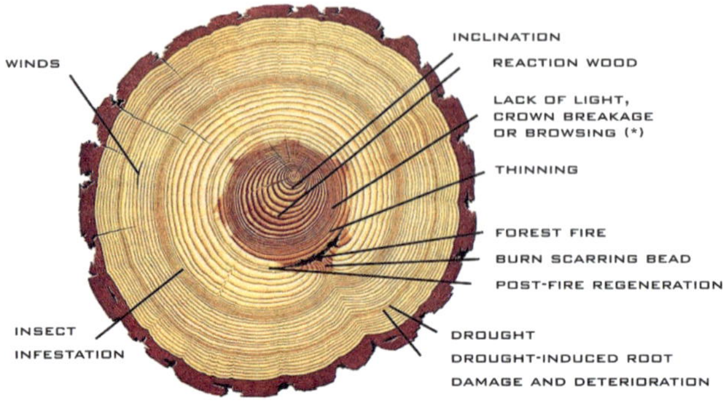

* Browsing[viii]

MEMORY
BY RICHARD FEYNMAN

https://www.facebook.com/reel/2139632166872027

4.4.1 Memory

The structure of reality is naturally persistent. Knowledge persists, engraved into the structure of reality, indexed by time.

In addition, elements of the structure of reality are modeled, interpreted and persisted through auxiliary memories, which are themselves also typically recorded in matter, such as biological or magnetic memories.

Knowledge is the structure of reality and knowing one of its element, is to know its structure, operation, relations, behavior, and constraints, every aspect of this element, much more than just its simple description.

Learning means analyzing and experimenting a reality in order to gain a better understanding of its structure and operation. See Learning, below.

Knowledge models processed by thought, anchor awareness of the structure of aspects of the reality of interest. In practice, knowledge models what it identifies about the structure of reality, or a subset thereof.

Nothing is lost, nothing is gained, everything transforms, and time indexes change. The image above shows how a dead tree that still teaches its history and that of its environment, through its existence.

DNA, for example, manages unequaled knowledge and shines through ability to memorize, reproduce, transmit, create beings and more, but also through its architecture, refinement and collaboration.

The structure of each element of reality constitutes a knowledge resource. See also *section 6.1.2 Resource*, as well as some examples, in the appendix, *section 9.2.1 Nature* and *9.2.1.7 Memory*.

 © 2023 Consonance Publishing

4.4.2 Learning

Learning is the process of Acquiring Knowledge.

LEARNING IS THE ART OF MEETING
ALBERT JACQUARD

Acquiring knowledge happens by experiencing reality's structure and operation, enabling their analysis, modeling and absorption (knowledge).

INCREASING KNOWLEDGE REDUCES ENTROPY

Learning can be achieved in two ways, or a combination thereof:

- **Direct learning**: the most complete approach, learning by experience, practice, experimentation, inference and modeling, through direct interaction with the structure and operation of the target reality.
- **Indirect learning**: through study, exchange, learning from others' experience, through shared information, projected from existing models. This learning approach typically requires anchoring from direct experimentation and comes in combinations of:
    - **Interactive**: through interaction with experienced entities, guide, mentor
    - **Deferred**: through artifacts like documents, models, books

IN ITS RACE WITH ENTROPY,
EVOLUTION LEARNS, IN ORDER TO BETTER STRUCTURE

Learning through informational artifacts (e.g. book, video) is often the most accessible and typically optimizes subsequent experimentation, which is still required to ensure effective knowledge (reality structure) absorption.

	LEARNING BY RICHARD FEYNMAN https://www.facebook.com/reel/885089097458062

© 2023 Consonance Publishing

OURS MAY BECOME THE FIRST CIVILIZATION DESTROYED
NOT BY THE POWER OF OUR ENEMIES
BUT BY THE IGNORANCE OF OUR TEACHERS
AND THE DANGEROUS NONSENSE
THEY ARE TEACHING OUR CHILDREN

IN AN AGE OF ARTIFICIAL INTELLIGENCE
THEY ARE CREATING ARTIFICIAL STUPIDITY

THOMAS SOWELL

Learning is a key aspect of knowledge processing. Artificial processors can benefit from following the natural model and taking advantage of their evolving knowledge backgrounds, as well as external (sensory and motor) and internal (metabolic) knowledge stream processing.

Machine learning is an important component of today's AI[ix]. Based on information processing rather than knowledge, today, machine learning is used in the context of massive AI, assisted or guided by a large or very large human contribution and is therefore subject to bias, not to mention intellectual property issues.

Today's massive AI is called upon to control all human support systems, including for information, undue biases pose unresolved challenges and intellectual property remains the main human differentiator and advantage.

Yet, nature favors the flexibility and resilience of modular structures, in dynamic networks, rather than monoliths and dinosaurs.

Like natural knowledge processors, the artificial ones are designed to learn from their interaction with the outside world, as well as from the operation and management of their knowledge metabolism. From a core, a DNA and basic training, each processor's metabolism evolves its knowledge background through experience and collaboration.

Injected learning, as in today's AI, remains useful, but artificial processors must be able to develop and evolve their autonomous learning, experience and knowledge, starting from inherited core, always in reference, at the the root of their evolving knowledge background.

Metabolic processes are determining for learning, as they are responsible for the evolution of the processor's knowledge background, and therefore for the correlation, integration and transformation of knowledge resources into the processor's knowledge background.

See also *section 7: Impacts*.

 © 2023 Consonance Publishing

4.4.3 Problem

Strategic opportunities to contribute to evolution, problems represent perceptions, a view of the mind, on a situation.

The perception of a problem is a signal from the subconscious to the conscious, indicating that some solution exists for a given situation and that the perceiving processor can contribute to resolving it.

If no solution exists, there is no problem, only a situation. The Andromeda galaxy will collide with the Milky Way. The event is astronomical, but not a problem, for lack of a potential solution.

On the other hand, getting out of a subway for an important meeting, and it's raining and the umbrella won't open, there is a problem to solve quickly, and a variety of solutions are available.

A problem only really exists in the minds of those who can and wish to help solve it, while for the rest of us, it remains a situation.

Yet problems are the key to happiness, if we listen and seize the opportunity. Solving a problem triggers the secretion of happiness hormones and the satisfaction of actually contributing to evolution. In collaboration, problem solving also increases solidarity between contributors.

Evolution fruits & tools, problems are natural indicators guiding knowledge processor intention & energy towards the realization of existence's meaning.[x]

The detection, the feeling of an imminent problem, which rapidly evolves into stress and perhaps dismay at the problem and its complexity, summons all components to get to work, resolve the problem, and enjoy the gratification.

The key is to understand & resolve problems, without making new ones.

Some processes enable effective problem understanding & resolution, including:

Approach	The *scientific approach* loops on: doubt, observation, analysis, hypothesis, evaluation, and challenge, to progressively evolve understanding and knowledge
Causality	In a strictly causal context, problems can only be resolved through effectively understanding and resolving *root causes*
Division	Powering entropy, division enables problem decomposition, required for resolution. Divide & Conquer. See Entropy and Asymmetry, above.

KNOW HOW TO SOLVE EVERY PROBLEM THAT HAS BEEN SOLVED

RICHARD FEYNMAN

4.4.4 INFORMATION

A communication tool (See section 5.4 Communication*), information is the more or less structured and arbitrary set of symbols and values exchanged through any media types.*

Some text-based examples of information include:

INFORMATION	DESCRIPTION
"25"	Value (number)
"PETE"	Identifier (could be a value)
"PETE=25"	Property (assign a value to an identifier)
"PETE : AGE=25 MASS=55"	Collection (assign 2 properties to an identifier)
"THE KEY IS ON THE TABLE"	Value (sentence)

Fundamentally, with information, everything is a symbol, or a symbol sequence, including values and identifiers. The distinctions lie in conventions and traditions modeled in codes and languages, each with its own lexicon, syntax and grammar, defining the potential combinatorial for each context, between values and identifiers.

Information serves communication and formalization, essential to collective operation (collaboration). Communication is based on sharing informational artifacts like messages and documents, between senders and receivers, roles reserved for advanced, natural or artificial knowledge-processors. In any case, information encodes shared content.

Senders project resource or model aspects from their respective knowledge background, under any set of criteria, into an informational view to be shared, with receivers that then need to interpret the information, infer proper corresponding knowledge resources, to integrate them into their respective knowledge background.

Current IT systems and regulations only consider information and most often, the appearance of information.

Processing knowledge processes information, in the context of knowledge, which provides meaning and relationships, enabling the effective exchange of knowledge resources between processors.

 © 2023 Consonance Publishing

4.4.5 Differences

KNOWLEDGE VS INFORMATION

Knowledge and information remain quite different. Understanding the differences and relationships between them, impacts their respective computerizing, in addition to contributing to a better grasp of the stakes.

4.4.5.1 Hierarchy

First, understanding the hierarchy between major knowledge services:

KNOWLEDGE PROCESSING MANAGES KNOWLEDGE SHARING, WHICH USES COMMUNICATION TO EXCHANGE INFORMATION

4.4.5.2 Structure

Knowledge includes at least:

- Archetypes, models and knowledge structures
- Qualified relationships[xi] between resources
- Processing networks of qualified relationships
- Continuous optimization of resources and processing (metabolism)
- Dynamic integration, correlation and classification
- Meaning, purpose and significance
- Ontological integration
- Governance tools, rules, constraints and indicators
- Security and governance management
- History, logging and tracking
- Communication for sharing and coordination
- Information, which it processes and produces through projection
- Knowledge on knowledge or meta-knowledge (meta-cognition), the consciousness engine

Knowledge is meaning, correlation, understanding and resolution.

INFORMATION ENCODES - KNOWLEDGE KNOWS

UNDERSTANDING ENABLES

© 2023 Consonance Publishing

4.4.5.3 INTERACTION

Knowledge & information are reciprocally linked through the projection and inference of knowledge resources:

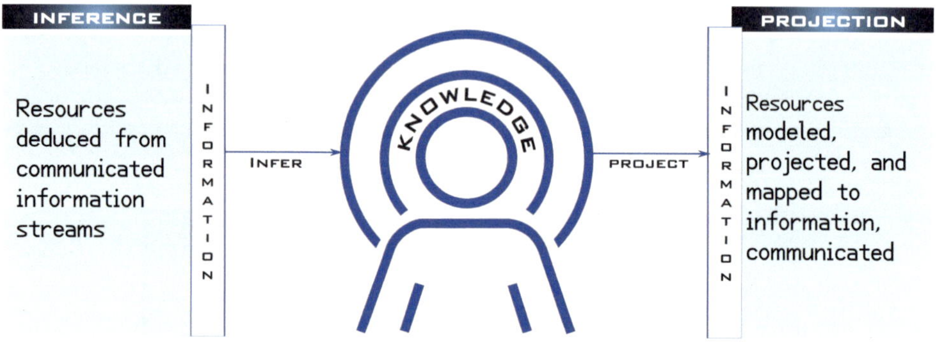

The projection and inference processes operating between knowledge and information can be relatively complex. Fortunately, for humans, knowledge processing is intuitive and typically subconscious.

Computerizing them requires more specific understanding of their operation.

4.4.5.4 OPERATION

Knowledge and information processing differ in many ways, including:

ASPECT	INFORMATION	KNOWLEDGE
CONVENTIONS	Conventions & arbitrary processing limit effective integration, management and governance	Natural model and principles, with qualified relationship driven processing
PROCESS	Convention, arbitrary	Naturally dynamic, intuitive, sustained, evolving, integrated
STANDARDS	Protocols, architecture, communication	Can be better standardized from its natural model, qualified relationships management, dynamic classification
APPLICATIONS	Current applications	Collaboration, sharing, intelligence, judgment, governance, in depth security

© 2023 Consonance Publishing

4.5 INTELLIGENCE

INTELLIGENCE IS THE KNOWLEDGE PROCESSING ABILITY

PROCESSING KNOWLEDGE IS EVOLVING IT

INTELLIGENCE
1. THINKING
2. MIND
3. SUBCONSCIOUS
4. CONSCIOUSNESS
5. CONGRUENCE
6. REFLEX
7. DISCIPLINE
8. FEELING
9. INTUITION
10. FREEDOM
11. SCIENCE

Attempts to define the term "intelligence" are more often simply lists of potential use cases. *Section 9.2.2 AI* provides ChatGPT's attempts at defining *9.2.2.2 Intelligence* and *9.2.2.3 Artificial Intelligence*, as non-definition examples.

Yet, simply, *intelligence is the ability to process knowledge.*

> **INTELLIGENCE IS THE SOLITARY FORCE TO EXTRACT FROM THE CHAOS OF ONE'S OWN LIFE A FISTFUL OF LIGHT, SUFFICIENT TO SHED SOME A LITTLE FURTHER THAN ONE'S SELF**
>
> CHRISTIAN BOBI

Knowledge processors, be they human, system or other, need to know how to recognize, acquire, analyze, model, understand, classify, organize, integrate, optimize, correlate, deepen, secure, exploit, trace, share..., knowledge resources.

> **INTELLIGENCE IS NOT WHAT WE KNOW, AS MUCH AS WHAT WE DO WHEN WE DON'T KNOW**
>
> JEAN PIAGET

In the natural and well proven knowledge processing architecture model, intelligence processes knowledge-resource streams:

- **Internal streams (metabolism)**: thought, continuous knowledge background processing: analyze, classify, correlate, integrate, validate, secure, evolve
- **External streams (Interaction)**: outside world interaction, such as learning, motorization (action), processing, sharing and collaboration
  - **Sensory** Streams (input), enable inferring knowledge resources
  - **Motor** Streams (output), enable projecting knowledge resources

Relative and correlative, fueled by experience, learning, rigor and creativity, intelligence is a determining catalyst for evolution and improvement.

Intelligence compares, qualifying, without granularity constraints.

Qualification, the fundamental intelligence operation, results from comparison

COMPARE (A, B) => Q

Each processor continually evolves (metabolism) its knowledge background, enriching and optimizing it from experience and shared streams, whose processing is relative to the processor's knowledge background.

IN A STRICTLY CAUSAL / RELATIVE CONTEXT QUALIFICATION MANAGEMENT IS KEY					
pp	*p*	*mp*	*mf*	*f*	*ff*

More so, in reality, each knowledge resource is involved in qualified relationships, each with engagements, rights, responsibilities, and others.

Human knowledge intelligence are intuitive and subconscious.

Developing intelligent systems that effectively process internal and external knowledge-resource streams, requires a deep operational and technical grasp of the related natural phenomena, starting with knowledge and intelligence.

For those who may not have this requirement for such a scientific understanding may not be required, this understanding remains relevant and beneficial, for knowledge, life, as for evolving education, for example.

	THE SEVEN LEVELS OF THOUGHT, LEARNING AND INTELLIGENCE BY RICHARD FEYNMAN https://www.facebook.com/reel/26014409878247973	1. Memorization 2. Comprehension 3. Application 4. Correlation 5. Judgment 6. Creation 7. Meta-cognition

Section 9.2.1 Nature presents a few examples of intelligence in nature, like:

	BBC SPIDER https://www.youtube.com/watch?v=nlRkwuAcUd4

© 2023 Consonance Publishing

4.5.1 Thinking

Thinking is exercising intelligence, processing and evolving knowledge.

In a broad sense, thinking is processing knowledge. More commonly, perhaps, and narrowly, the verb "to think" often refers primarily to certain processes associated with the more conscious part of the mind. Unless otherwise stated, the term is used here in its broader sense.

Section 4.5.3 Subconscious, below, also considers the intense activity of thought during sleep, as evidenced by dreams, for example.

In the common sense, thinking is typically an awareness of aspects of the processor's metabolic processes, i.e., background processes that continuously validate, correlate, refine, develop, and evolve the knowledge background of the processor, whether human or system.

4.5.2 Mind

The mind encompasses all the operating processes of a knowledge processor (human or system). The mind is the energy driving each processor to optimize its knowledge & intelligence (metabolism), process its sensory and motor streams, its ethics code and value scale, as well as the effectiveness of its contribution to evolution.

The mind is relative and, indeed, can only define absolute or infinite as that which is not relative, i.e. an entirely relative definition. Evolution fruit & tool, the mind gets meaning from its contribution to evolution, from the meaning of existence. See *section 4.3.4 Meaning*.

With its relative autonomy, however, the mind also benefits from a clear understanding of powerful natural indicators such as the Happiness and Transformation axes, for example. Fond of knowledge, intelligence, structure and beauty, the mind feeds on evolution. Knowledge processors provide it with an interface to outside world.

We can naturally divide the human mind's operation, into major functional blocks such as: conscious, subconscious, reflex, will, ego, sensory, motor and others. See below. Mostly subconscious, the mind also includes its conscious operation. Consciousness and subconsciousness are meta-cognition applications.

Mind
by Richard Feynman

https://www.facebook.com/reel/1897944314145178

© 2023 Consonance Publishing

4.5.3 Subconscious

The operation of the mind is essentially subconscious. Even the operation of the conscious mind is mostly subconscious. As the main operational block of the mind, the subconscious refers to all subconscious processes of the mind.

The term "subconscious" refers to normally unconscious operations, but which could be partially or temporarily conscious, depending on a number of factors. Typically, when the conscious mind presents a clear request to the subconscious, it will grant appropriate access to the required streams, for the time needed. Consciousness is expensive

Many processes, such as learning, reflexes or habits, combine the action of both conscious and subconscious mind functions. The congruence and synergy between all mind processes, is key to the processor's effectiveness, as to intelligence.

The conscious mind, considered below, is in fact a tool, an extension, of the subconscious, a set of mostly subconscious processes that orchestrate, interaction (sensor, motor) with the outside world and whose main function is to filter, adapt, and prepare for inference, integration, or projection.

In most species, for example, the subconscious regularly puts the conscious to sleep. The reverse typically seems rather much more definitive.

Responsible for maintaining vital functions, the subconscious mind operates continuously, processing knowledge from its background and from its experience interacting with the outside world.

© 2023 Consonance Publishing

In addition to sharing knowledge through sensory & motor streams, each processor evolves through experience and a set of metabolic parallel processes integrating, optimizing and developing its knowledge background.

When awake, the conscious mind makes heavy demands on the subconscious, occupying part of the available bandwidth and delaying other processes.

This is why, in humans, for example, the subconscious regularly induces the conscious mind to sleep for about a third of each and every day, allowing it to devote more resources to other required knowledge-metabolism processes.

PEOPLE WILL DO ANYTHING, NO MATTER HOW ABSURD IN ORDER TO AVOID FACING THEIR OWN SOULS

CARL GUSTAV JUNG

It's not surprising, then, that in the first moments of awakening, the conscious mind can occasionally catch a brief glimpse of the still feverish activity of the subconscious mind. Understanding very little from it, the conscious tries to interpret, model, illustrate and project what it understood in what appears to be a dream.

UNTIL YOU MAKE THE UNCONSCIOUS CONSCIOUS IT WILL DIRECT YOUR LIFE AND YOU WILL CALL IT FATE

CARL GUSTAV JUNG

4.5.4 Conscious

The conscious mind is an integration layer responsible for monitoring and coordinating the interaction between the mind and the external world, the first layer of which is often the processor's own body/system.

Based on subconscious priorities, the conscious mind can monitor otherwise subconscious processes, either from metabolism and the operational context, or from interaction through sensory and motor streams.

As the mind's representative to the outside world, well connected to the subconscious and its great integrating processes, such as the Self or Ego, the conscious articulates the "I" in each processor, presenting an integrated vision of the processor, enabling it to interact as entity within the whole.

The conscious mind's strategic position makes it an important contributor to the analysis and breakdown of problems, as well as to reflex & habit learning, development and triggering.

Main external stream (interaction) filter, for the subconscious mind, on one side, the conscious mind infers knowledge resources from sensory streams, and on the other side, projects knowledge resources through motor streams, for expression and behavior.

The conscious mind rapidly converts, qualifies, processes and prepares the external stream's large data volumes for communication to/from the subconscious mind, metabolism and knowledge background.

Responsible for deep knowledge integration and processing, the subconscious mind only knows and processes knowledge resources.

Consciousness
by Richard Feynman
https://www.facebook.com/reel/2029425094270557

 © 2023 Consonance Publishing

4.5.5 Congruency

Every day, every activity can combine conscious and subconscious functions.

These activities, such as feeling, perceiving, moving, or communicating, typically combine several functions that must work together in the most harmonious and congruent way to ensure the best possible results.

Each resource must ensure congruency & synergy for itself and recursively for its components. Like for other resources, the mind maintains congruency & synergy for itself and recursively for its components. Everything must also be designed to adapt to evolving contexts.

Congruency constitutes a desired balance, never perfectly achieved, yet indispensable. Without congruency, the components work against each other. The processor's congruency also depends on its metabolic processes, as congruency applies to all involved resources.

Part of congruency also relies on resource orchestration, according to context, resources, uses, rights, etc., but above all on the qualified relationships that define behaviors, among other things.

Orchestration is based on the clear articulation of operations, triggers, filters, conditions, objectives, and required modes of operation.

It seems interesting to consider the collaboration between the conscious and the subconscious minds through the following use cases:

SYNERGY

**THE TOTAL NUMBER OF MINDS IN THE UNIVERSE IS ONE.
CONSCIOUSNESS IS A SINGULARITY
THAT PHASES WITHIN ALL BEINGS**

INTERNET

© 2023 Consonance Publishing

4.5.5.1 Resolve

Trying to solve a "complex" problem, every knowledge processor, can benefit by allowing its conscious mind analyze, break down and understand all problem parameters, causes and aspects, before going to sleep to let the subconscious mind's metabolic processes perform optimally.

Awareness of the problem's structure, aspects and details provides optimal request, context and parameters for the best subconscious metabolic performance and resolution.

If, on awakening, the solution is still not clear, this means that the awareness process is incomplete, as the subconscious has not had all required elements, and another cycle is required.

The subconscious is the best complex problems solver, while the conscious mind provides the best interface to the external world.

4.5.5.2 Wake-up

The deeply sleep-deprived, with little time to rest, and no alarm-clock to help prevent missing a crucial meeting, one can call upon its subconscious by consciously considering the importance of waking up at the right time, three times, long and deep enough for the subconscious to setup for this.

Clear, and repeated, awareness and intention provide the time that the subconscious requires to register the request properly and understand the stakes, before putting the conscious into deep sleep (REM).

The subconscious will wake up the conscious at the right time, without fault, possibly ahead of time by a few minutes at the most, just to allow morning fog to dissipate.

© 2023 Consonance Publishing

4.5.6 Reflex

Most behavioral processes, whether conscious or subconscious, use repetition: pulse, walking, metabolism, work, habits, expression and so on.

For the purpose here, the term "reflex" includes inherited, and acquired reflexes, as well as programmable habits and automation.

The domains and levels of incrustation may vary for each, but principles remain.

Repetition, like its heirs: reflex and habit, is a fundamental principle (corrugation) essential to knowledge processing and intelligence in general.

Fruits and tools of evolution, reflex functions are natural processes that define, manage, support, promote, evaluate, update and use repeated processes. Globally, they are referred to as the mind's reflex "area" or function.

The conditioned reflex concept is for the conscious mind to program some reflex or automation into the subconscious and to associate its execution to triggers, filters, conditions and parameters.

The main objective is to record a sequence to replay it many times, then freeing the conscious mind from playback/execution for concentrating on other outside world interface related tasks. At execution, the programmed automation is then handled by the subconscious, The conscious mind can still intervene, as required.

As programmable automation, reflexes are the second most important productivity factor, after collaboration. Reflex management is therefore a strategic component of intelligence.

Inherited reflexes come from a basic core transmitted at the outset - genetic background, for example. A large number of reflexes are acquired or developed through the processor's experience and life cycle.

See also *section 6.2.3.3 Metabolism*.

The learning, developing or conditioning a new reflex follows a certain pattern, requiring direct intervention from the conscious mind, to adapt to each specific context.

In principle, developing a new reflex, the conscious mind must:

STEP	TASK
PLAN	1.Establish a precise sequence conditioning plan
STRATEGY	2.Determine appropriate learning strategies
AWARENESS	3.Become deeply aware of each element or aspect
DISCIPLINE	4.Ensure slow, articulated practice of each sequence step
REPETITION	5.Repeat this practice until the sequence is automated
QUALITY	6.Ensure continuous quality assurance, all levels

Practice integrates reflexes, making them subconscious and intuitive. To do so, the subconscious mind requires knowledge of all steps, details and nuances of the reflex structure, in order to record, model and correlate them optimally. It also especially requires "sleep" intervals to metabolize all elements at full power.

Reflex execution is initiated by associated triggers. A trigger can be associated with more than one reflex, a reflex can have several triggers, and a reflex can be a trigger for others.

Automated behavioral sequences become reflexes and can, like walking for example, be performed virtually without conscious intervention.

The processor is responsible for managing its acquired reflex life cycles: definition, conditioning, triggering, interruption, use, evolution, retirement.

Effective and useful, reflexes contribute to increased productivity, at the price of an initial learning and coordination investment.

Typically, a determined human takes an average 21 days of daily practice (frequency, duration, structure, intensity), with all the required sleep, to allow the subconscious mind to ensure the complete recording, That is when reflex starts to operate subconsciously.

The work of musicians, craftsmen, assembly-line workers and others is largely based on the systematic use of large quantities of reflexes.

Modifying an acquired reflex requires the conscious mind to fight the the incrustation of the previous reflex in the subconscious, "naturally" returning until the new version as been repeated more often than the old.

 © 2023 Consonance Publishing

4.5.7 DISCIPLINE

Bridging between the objective and its achievement, essential to reflex conditioning and management, as well as to most operations, discipline enables effective freedom, by providing the means, methods & tools required to fully instantiate the selected choice.

4.5.8 FEELING

Feelings are messages from the subconscious mind and body (through the subconscious mind), to the conscious mind.

EMOTIONS ARE TRAJECTORY-ADJUSTMENT SYSTEMS
POSITIVE, YOU'RE ON COURSE. NEGATIVE, SOMETHING'S GONE ASTRAY
DR JORDAN B. PETERSON

4.5.9 INTUITION

Intuition signals subconscious mind responses to conscious mind requests.

INTUITION IS THE EAR OF THE SOUL

To provide this response, the processor's subconscious mind analyzes, qualifies and correlates in depth, its inherited and acquired knowledge background.

EXPERIENCE & CONGRUENCE ENABLE INTUITIVE PRECISION & RELEVANCE

In a strictly causal & relative universe, where doubt is the key to knowledge, in congruence and symbiosis with all mind components, including all of its knowledge-background, intuition remains the most reliable reference for each processor, as it results from :

- Depth and refinement of knowledge and processes
- Access to the complete knowledge-background and qualified relationships
- Experience history, also recorded in its knowledge-background

4.5.10 FREEDOM

Freedom is the discipline required to ensure the full realization of choices.

- **Potential freedom**: Set of potential options. Choice is the selection of required option(s).
- **Effective freedom**: Realization of the selection. Discipline to take all required means to successfully achieve the full realization of the selection, including rejecting all other options
- **Freedom constraint**: Freedom is only restricted by the required respect of others, their freedom, life, ecosystem and evolution

© 2023 Consonance Publishing

4.5.11 Science

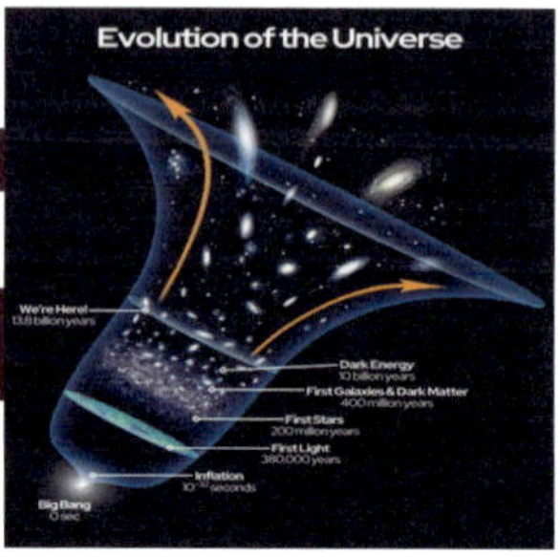

THE ART OF DOUBT

SCIENCE ADVANCES ONE FUNERAL AT A TIME
MAX PLANCK

Doubt is the key to knowledge, as it guides the scientific process which is the most effective way to increase and evolve knowledge and understanding.

The scientific approach main characteristic lies in its endless loop over the principles of doubt, observation, analysis, evaluation, hypothesis & challenge. Not only does the approach start from doubt, doubt guides its every step.

While doubt is never completely resolved, probabilities vary and adjust through the different stages and evaluations.

Other problem-solving principles are typically integrated into the scientific approach, such as :

- **Causality**: finding, understanding and resolving root causes
- **Division**: breaking down problems and solving sub-problems

See also *section 4.4.3 Problem*, as well as:

	SCIENCE: ART OF DOUBT BY RICHARD FEYNMAN https://www.facebook.com/reel/2578190867149439 3

 © 2023 Consonance Publishing

5 Collaboration

Collaboration, solidarity and evolution engine, main knowledge-processor activity, is defined by a tacit or explicit agreement between collaborators, wishing to increase their productivity and solidarity, in the course of their contribution to evolution. The agreement typically defines exchanges, sharing, partnerships, realizations and distributions required by the collaboration.

COMPETITION IS THE LAW OF THE JUNGLE
COLLABORATION IS THE LAW OF CIVILIZATION
PETER KROPOTKIN

Each processor's contribution repeatedly passes through its own processing channel with its three main knowledge processing chains:

Acquisition	Metabolism	Expression
Collect, filter, transform sensory streams (input)	knowledge-background processing (Internal)	Project through motor streams (output)

The success of collaboration is typically proportional to the affinity of the objectives, motivation and strategies of the collaborators.

The primary sources of motivation for collaboration, the productivity and solidarity gains serve to achieve common and complementary objectives.

THE ONLY VALUABLE COMPETITION IS AGAINST ONE'S OWN SELF
ALBERT JACQUARD

Resulting productivity and mutual prosperity growth also generates solidarity, the unifying force and trust foundation between collaborators, helps ciment their communities.

Collaboration => greatest source & factor of:			
Productivity	Prosperity	Solidarity	Evolution

See also *section 9.3.3 Collaboration*.

Refining knowledge and intelligence, societies naturally organize themselves around collaboration and solidarity through structures such as: family, team, community, enterprise, network, nation, etc., collaborating in all fields.

The source and main driver of productivity and solidarity, knowledge and intelligence throttle, collaboration is shared experience.

The natural process hierarchy distinguishes the logical processing layers between knowledge and information, as well as their interweaving:

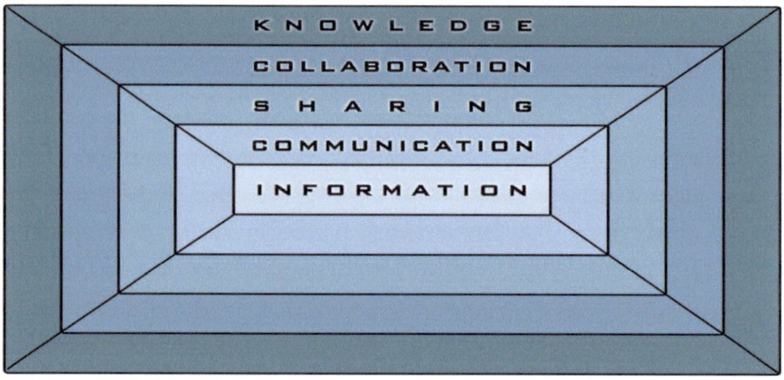

INFORMATION	*IS A*	**COMMUNICATION**	*TOOL*
COMMUNICATION	*IS A*	**SHARING**	*TOOL*
SHARING	*IS A*	**COLLABORATION**	*TOOL*
COLLABORATION	*IS A*	**KNOWLEDGE**	*TOOL*

To convert between knowledge and information, each unidirectional transmission requires the use of two sophisticated, subjective and essentially inverse processes, one on transmission and the other on reception.

Considered more specifically in *section 5.4.2 Conversion*, these processes are subjective and relate to each processor's knowledge background. They are:

- **Projection**

  Based on its knowledge background, from a viewpoint on a model section, a processor projects aspects of a knowledge model, through a perspective to determine how the projection is mapped, to a codified informational artifact or document

- **Inference**

  Receivers decode and interpret the information artifact, inferring knowledge resources, to metabolize (qualify, correlate, integrate) to their respective knowledge background.

 © 2023 Consonance Publishing

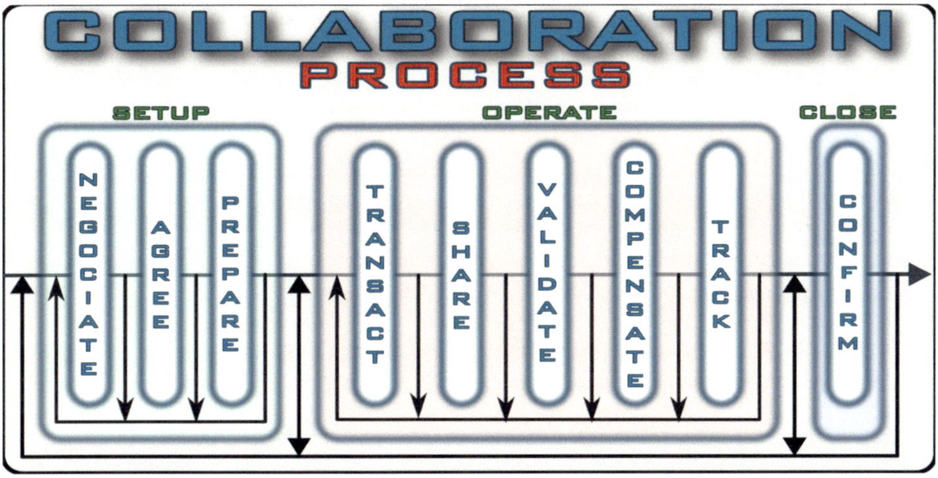

5.1 Operation

Collaboration typically combines several stages in three main phases: set-up, operation and close-out, as illustrated above.

Each step and phase can be repeated and, for example, a collaboration could be set up and closed once, while including several sharing and exchange operations.

- **Set up**
  - **Negotiation:** Negotiate the collaboration conditions
  - **Agreement:** Agree to collaborate terms
  - **Preparation:** Prepare to carry out the collaboration.
- **Operate**
  - **Transaction:** Perform required transaction(s)
  - **Sharing:** Carry out sharing(s)
  - **Validation:** Validate compliance on both sides
  - **Compensation:** Ensure appropriate compensation distribution
  - **Follow-up:** Ensure quality and tracking the sharing(s)
- **Close**
  - **Confirmation:** Adjust and confirm collaboration completion.

© 2023 Consonance Publishing

5.2 Prerequisite

Successful collaboration has a number of prerequisites, including some strategic and structuring intelligence functions, such as judgment and knowledge-background compatibility.

5.2.1 Compatibility

Processors are all different, each with their own heritage, experience and knowledge background.

For each processor, it's knowledge background represents its analysis, synthesis & understanding reference grid, its interpretation matrix.

Collaboration requires planning, definition, framework, management.

The compatibility of intentions and of knowledge-backgrounds is determining, This compatibility enables friends to understand each other well, often with very few words. This compatibility is primarily based on combination of similarity and complementarity:

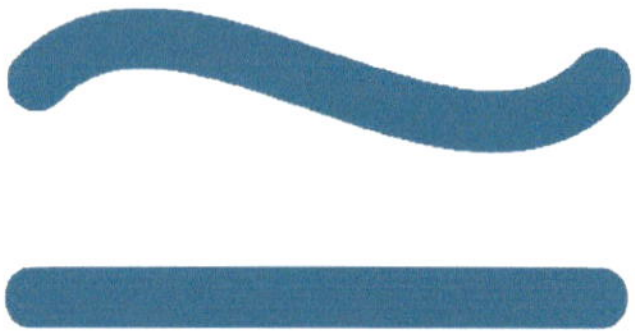	• **Similarity** of intentions and of knowledge backgrounds ensures a common reference base, which in turn fosters the shared understanding that is vital to successful collaboration. First indispensable factor to compatibility, similarity alone is not enough.
	• Also indispensable to compatibility, **complementary** of intentions and of knowledge-backgrounds provide crucial foundations for collaboration and collaborative work, as well as for the associated motivation and solidarity.

Compatibility between collaborators and the success of their collaborations rest largely on the abundance and balance between similarity and complementarity.

As the number of processors increases, compatibility principles and management become more important.

For humans as for intelligent systems, the main compatibility enabling factors include inheritance, education and training.

 © 2023 Consonance Publishing

5.2.2 JUDGMENT

Essential to evolution, *judgment is the art of making the right choices*. Judgment is a foundation of intelligence, essential for collaboration.

Operating at all levels, several fundamental processes underpin judgment, including two especially important ones, tolerance and prioritization, briefly considered below.

Although different in their application, these judgment processes aim to nuance (qualify) evaluations, choices, and actions from complementary viewpoints, through the analysis, processing, and correlation of resource networks from the processor's knowledge-background via the qualified relationships that structure them.

5.2.2.1 TOLERANCE

Even with similar and compatible knowledge-backgrounds, intelligence must apply appropriate tolerance, especially when faced with inference and modeling processes, which strongly rely on different and imperfect knowledge backgrounds.

The key is not on the table, but we suppose it could be around perhaps, or in another room … What's more, the friend was talking about one key on a table, but, rather, there are several hanging on the wall.

In this case, it's tolerance to the imprecision of information, in the face of the dual process of modeling and inference.

Fortunately, mutual knowledge background awareness made it possible, for example, to think that the neighbor might have forgotten that he had put the key on the hook, or it might have been his partner who did, for example. Either way, tolerance was appropriate and necessary.

5.2.2.2 PRIORITIZATION

As with tolerance, prioritization is a sophisticated, strategic, global, weighting process, based on qualified relationship management. The objective is different. Evaluation is used to qualify according to criteria, rather than to manage imprecision.

Qualifying all processes, natural, intuitive, prioritization manifests itself everywhere in our lives. The fading details of memories is evidence of their diminishing prioritization. But, even as they fade, they can be recalled, willfully or under hypnosis, for example. Their priority evolves.

5.3 Sharing

Sharing is a step in a collaboration, under an explicit or implicit agreement, For the owner of a resource (emitter) wishes to share access to it with potential users (receivers) who want that access, in exchange for compensation.

Collaborations and shared resources types vary and can target ideas, messages, documents, goods and services, physical or virtual.

Owners and users agree on conditions and compensations associated to the sharings..

Donation remains an extreme case of sharing, since the agreement are often tacit and provides for neither conditions nor compensation. For other cases or types of sharing, conditions, constraints, compensation and follow-up must be considered, as well as:

- Content classification
- Context, objectives, strategies, sharing schedules
- Parties involved, respective constraints and backgrounds
- Modes and means of communication and exchange
- Use of content
- Terms and conditions
- Monitoring content, usage and sharing
- Encryption and encryption key management
- Access security, integrity, confidentiality
- Compensation terms & processes, including
    - Usage-based invoicing
    - Micro-payments

Today, apart from giving, sharing is poorly supported, especially as the Internet is only partially secure and otherwise even less.

Without the required knowledge, qualified relationship and intelligence processing, information processing cannot support the dynamic classification and governance, indispensable to sharing security.

Knowledge processing can provide the required sharing support, including security, compensation, tracking and compliance.

See also *section 5.5 Security*.

 © 2023 Consonance Publishing

5.3.1 Process

A collaboration process may comprise several shares, depending on the terms of the associated agreement. Each of these shares is itself a process comprising various stages, typically like:

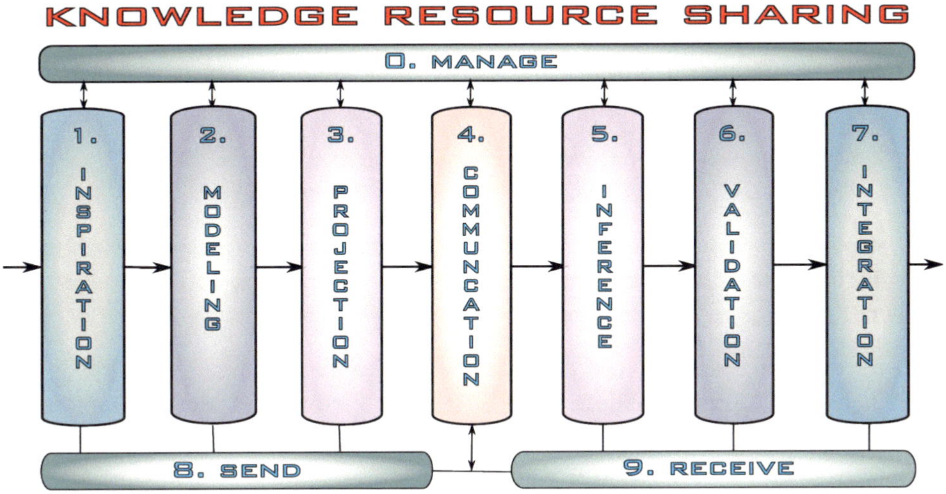

0. **Manage**: Agreement, contributors, process, log, history, notification
1. **Inspiration**: Articulate intentions, targets, purpose, roles, plan and strategies, relative to sender's knowledge-background
2. **Modeling**: Build, validate, approve the model in accordance with point #1
3. **Projection**: From a sender's viewpoint and knowledge-background, the sender projects model aspects through the required artifact-specific perspective
4. **Communication**: Encode, encrypt transfer, decrypt, decode, and confirm secure artifact transfer
5. **Inference**: In relation to its own knowledge-background, the receiver validates, interprets and infers corresponding knowledge resources, from received artifacts.
6. **Validation**: Parties validate that the inferred resources the receiver integrates to its knowledge background match the sender's projected resources, as well as conformance and completeness
7. **Integration**: The receiver integrates the new validated resources to its knowledge background and the sharing collects and distributes compensation
8. **Send**: Group and integrate emitting stages
9. **Receive**: Group and integrate receiving stages

The scope of each step depends on the specific contexts, but the success of the sharing process depends on the success of each and every step. Failure at one step typically leads to failure in sharing.

The diagram above summarizes a knowledge-resource sharing phase in the context of collaboration between a sender (#8) and a receiver (#9). Framed by an implicit or explicit agreement to collaborate, the parties coordinate (#0) each unidirectional sharing phase, the main steps of which are indicated here as ## 1-7.

Relative to the sender and its knowledge-background, steps ## 1, 2, and 3 aim to produce an informational artifact to be transmitted.

The pivotal for the phase, step #4 is responsible for the secure transmission of the artifact between the parties and constitutes an instance of unidirectional communication. See also *section 5.4 Communication*.

Relative to the receiver and its own knowledge-background, steps ## 5, 6, and 7 aim to infer, validate, and integrate, from the received artifact, knowledge resources corresponding to those projected by the sender.

Each side of the pivot (#4), both projection (#3) on transmission and inference (#5) on reception, are sophisticated and subjective steps, relative to the respective knowledge-backgrounds, and therefore especially delicate and strategic.

Sender and receiver are not limited to individuals and may each include several knowledge-processors, each with its own knowledge-background, this multi-subjectivity requires understanding and coordination (#0) in order to better structure and manage complexity and consistency.

As noted above, the actual complexity of each step and of the entire process depends on each specific context, but is rarely trivial and can easily be underestimated.

Section 5.4 Communication considers, for example, the relay (#4) between transmission and reception, as well as some implications of the differences between knowledge and information.

Effective and systematic management of qualified relationships quickly becomes essential for managing, combining, correlating, integrating, and securing projections, inferences, conventions, encoding, translations, and encryption in a context of knowledge-backgrounds, metabolisms, intentions, attention, and others, all complex, diverse, and hybrid (human-system).

© 2023 Consonance Publishing

5.3.2 VALUATION[XII]

Markets and economy are supported by a set of measures, technologies, standards, laws, controls, and other mechanisms working to ensure the equitable valuation of shared resources.

While *section 7.2.4.2 Transition* considers correlations between usage-value of a resource and its market or commercial value, this section focuses on the latter, foundational in a transactional compensated knowledge sharing economy.

In a grocery store where products on are displayed and freely accessible, everyone pays for what they take in accordance with the underlying social agreement supported by security and valuation measures, like: passing through checkouts, guards, doors, offices, barriers, managers, lawyers, police services, laws, prisons, insurances, cameras, phones and education, not to mention the potential humiliation and costs associated with trespassing them. These measures all serve to ensure the commercial value of the shared resources.

Similarly, developing an effective, prosperous, and sustainable knowledge economy requires the valuation and security of shared knowledge resources. Many factors affect the value of shared resources, but sharing security is an essential prerequisite. For all practical purposes, without adequate security, transactional value remains essentially zero.

As with the sharing of physical resources, the sharing of knowledge resources depends on its transactional and commercial infrastructure. The intelligent collaboration platforms that support this sharing are strategic components in the responsibility to ensure sustainable value.

Section 5.5 Security considers some of these aspects and associated technologies in more detail. The issue is not trivial, and intelligent sharing and collaboration platforms must at a minimum integrate systematic management of qualified relationships, as well as dynamic classification and governance, in addition to modern tracking, encryption, and steganography technologies.

The creation and ownership of knowledge resources are specifically human properties to which intelligent systems can provide strategic support for a prosperous knowledge economy.

© 2023 Consonance Publishing

5.4 Communication

Communication is the art and science of sharing information. Essential to collaboration and sharing, at first glance it seems simple, but in practice it is the most sophisticated and fragile of all common activities.

In principle, information is used to represent and encode views of knowledge resources for sharing. Strictly speaking, communication serves to transfer these views between senders and receivers.

More broadly, communication includes coding and decoding processes between knowledge resources and informational views, as well as ensuring the integrity of views across the various processes, media, and interpretations.

Introduced, in *section 5.3.1 Process*, as the sharing process linchpin, communication complexity deserves more attention, especially since it is responsible for materializing and dematerializing the typically more abstract knowledge resources into informational artifacts, while ensuring their integrity and the quality of their exchanges.

Humans learn to communicate naturally and intuitively, but in order to better develop effectively intelligent systems, it seems crucial to better grasp relevant aspects and challenges.

While *section 6 Artificial* considers knowledge resources representation, this section first considers the fundamental processes of modeling with its associated projection and inference conversion processes, between informational views and knowledge resource models, as well as ensuring content integrity through and through.

 © 2023 Consonance Publishing

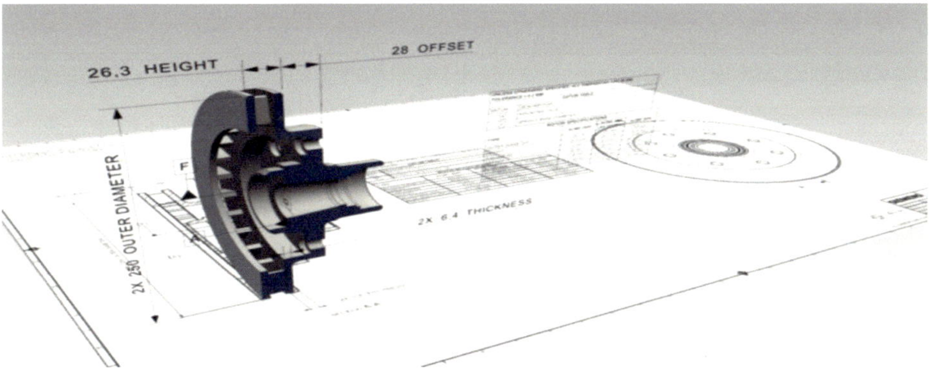

5.4.1 Modeling

Modeling represents knowledge resources, conceptually or otherwise, to enable them to be processed and shared. For sharing, models are imported through inference and exported through projection.

The model is the first formalization of a knowledge-resource, developed within the knowledge-processor's own knowledge-background.

The car driver, for example, a knowledge processor, drives the mental model of the vehicle. It is from this representation that he decides which muscles to invoke, since his mind has no direct access to the physical vehicle. It drives the mental model of the vehicle with its sensory & motor streams, through its model fo the current external reality.

	Reality Model by Richard Feynman https://www.facebook.com/reel/1163747052339762

An indispensable tool for knowledge processing, modeling enables representing, structuring, navigating and managing, as well as projecting knowledge models into views and artifacts required by communication, sharing and collaboration.

Senders build a model and project aspects of it from viewpoints, through perspectives, towards informational views, in artifacts to be shared. Receivers interpret artifacts to infer corresponding knowledge resources, in the light of their own knowledge-backgrounds. In addition, models :

- Reflect, articulate and document reality-structure element awareness
- Instantiate[xiii] the knowledge resources to be processed and shared
- Are crucial to knowledge management and evolution
- Form the foundations of communication.

5.4.2 Conversion

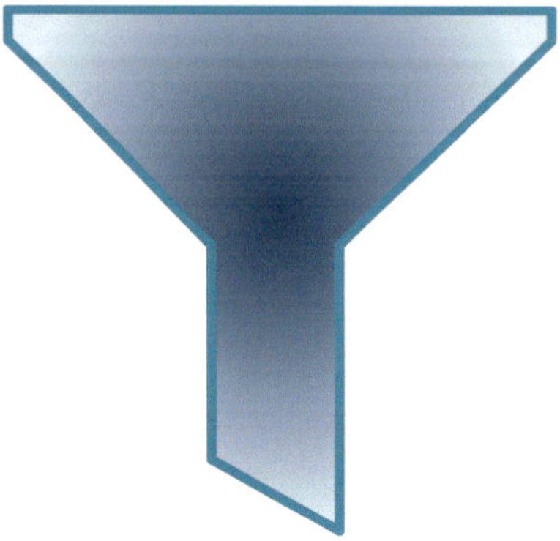

Knowledge processors process and model knowledge resources. The most systematic approach to sharing these models and resources, communication, requires the materialization of these knowledge resources into informational artifacts.

These artifacts can take a multitude of forms and potentially be adapted to all media types.

Regardless of the form or medium, knowledge models must be converted into information, i.e., sequences of symbols structured by grammars and conventions. Sounds, texts, illustrations, or other artifacts can then be shared and persisted.

Since the nature and structure of knowledge and information are very different, knowledge processors must convert aspects of their models during import and export using two sophisticated processes: projection (export) and inference (import):

- **Projection**: Enables a sender to export from its own knowledge-background, aspects of knowledge-resource models, into information artifacts
- **Inference**: Enables a receiver to import to its own knowledge-background, knowledge resources, from information artifacts

The three main phases of communication are:

Projection – Transmission – Inference

These subjective conversions, which are directly related to the specific knowledge background of each sender and receiver involved, play an important role in the communication process.

These conversions are integrated directly into the sensory and motor stream processing interfaces of each knowledge-processor.

Subjective and complex, they represent a significant source of errors affecting communication, sharing, and collaboration.

Their integrity requires significant quality control.

© 2023 Consonance Publishing

5.4.2.1 PROJECTION

Each processor instantiates or "materializes" subconscious knowledge resources into models that be used to manage and project into information streams of views and artifacts, required for sharing and communication.

Projection reduces dimensionality, as when a person's shadow is projected onto the wall or floor, for example, from 3D to 2D.

Model projection reduces content by using:

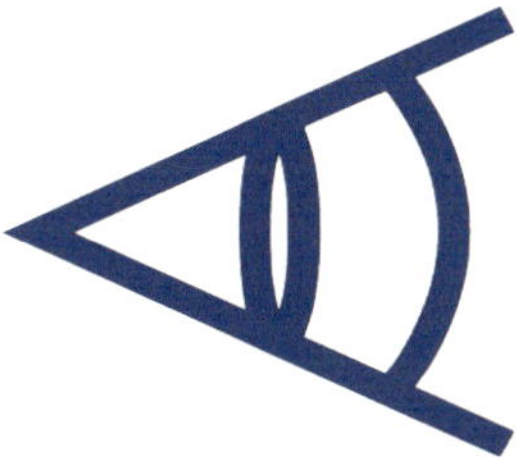

- **WHAT:** *Viewpoints,* or view angles, parametrize the selection of model aspects to project to the required views

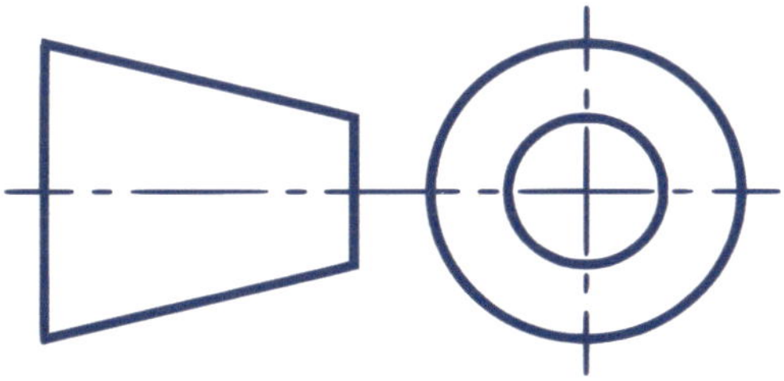

- **HOW:** *Perspectives* parametrize how view are to be produced, including type, format, view port, media, encoding, for example

To illustrate, for an activity or organization (model), a processor could assume a shareholder's viewpoint to project profitability, through a perspective of tables, graphs or reports, in two languages, assembled in PDF format, by language, for example.

The aim of projection is to impact the external world. Communication, along with sharing and collaboration effectively contribute.

Typically, some processors share knowledge around each shared view, each enriching and evolving its background.

Knowledge, like reality and its structure, is rich and profound, guided by the multitude of qualified relationships that connect all its elements.

Translating this complexity into information artifacts requires a drastic reduction in content. Artifacts can be multiplied, but the often complex projection must choose angles and points of view, areas of focus, compromises, and rely on the inference and processing capabilities of the receivers.

© 2023 Consonance Publishing

5.4.2.2 Inference

Inference is a sophisticated metabolic process that enables each processor (receiver) to deduce and infer, by correlation, integrating into its own knowledge background, knowledge resources that correspond to the resources projected through information selected, interpreted, decoded from received artifacts.

Inference makes it possible to instantiate, create and integrate new knowledge resources into a processor's background, based on contexts and conventions.

Inference increases dimensionality.

Parts of the processor's metabolism, correlation, deduction and inference operate continuously, across the entire prioritized knowledge background. See also *Section 6.2.3.3 Metabolism*.

In interaction, with rapid throughput and response times, dependent on a multitude of factors and contexts, a sophisticated process subject to error, failure and corruption, inference is a strategic step in communication.

In principle is that the content of exchanged artifacts can guide the receiver's mind through its inference process, enabling it in the reconstruction of corresponding knowledge resources, in relation to its own knowledge background, while assessing the relevance method of integrating them into it, validating each aspect and step in doing so.

ORDER	CHAOS

 © 2023 Consonance Publishing

5.4.3 Integrity

Ensuring the integrity of shared content is a fundamental aspect of communication, sharing and collaboration. Content integrity is also extended through security. See 5.5 Security.

Integrity is key at every step, but especially through communication, where integrity vulnerability diversity suggests an adapted operational approach.

At every step, communication is vulnerable to noise, error, imperfection, and attack. Each of these factors challenges shared content integrity, as well as of the actual communication results.

Challenges to integrity over the cascade of interdependent processes include:

- Knowledge resource model articulation based on the respective knowledge background of each emitter
- Model projection, from view points and angles selecting aspects to project, through perspectives a point of view, through a perspective that defines how to reduce and translate these aspects to adapt them to views rendered into informational artifacts
- Sophisticated subjectivity of choices and biases guiding both projection and inference conversion processes
- Arbitrary traditions, conventions, languages, coding and presentations required for communication
- Omnipresent errors, weaknesses, failings, jamming of used media and required conversions
- Malice, rivalries, approbations, corruption and natural entropy

Consequently, each level of each stage must provide adequate detection and corrective mechanisms to minimize share content aggressions. It is not surprising that these operations occupy a major part of the processing of artifacts transmission.

Integrity is a fundamental condition to sharing and collaboration. Its complexity requires knowledge and intelligence, supported by qualified relationships network management, as they define contexts ans applications. See also *section 9.3.7 Integrity*.

5.5 SECURITY

The *section 3 Key* example shows how managing shared content security, as well as the required trust between parties, is intrinsic to knowledge, and adapts dynamically as resources, contexts and knowledge backgrounds evolve.

Content-sharing security is built into and managed at the very heart of resources, structures and relationships. Dynamic classification, unlimited in granularity and intuitive for humans, is an indispensable tool in supporting sharing security.

Qualified relationship management, which supports dynamic classification, enables understanding the associations, constraints, contexts, participants, frames or values required for dynamic classification.

By helping to secure sharing, dynamic classification valuates intellectual property and lays the foundations for the knowledge economy.

Although strategic, dynamic classification is only one aspect of security and this section briefly considers a few more.

Key to sharing and collaboration, security is in fact a fundamental pillar of any successful economy.

5.5.1 AUTHENTICATION

A basic operation and the first step in the security operation process, authentication validates and confirms the identity of all parties apparently involved in a share, including each contributor, administrator or user. Access points are authentication points.

Several authentication approaches are available and can be combined. In the example in *section 3 Key*, neighbors combine sight, hearing and context to mutually recognize and validate identities.

In this example, for each of these approaches, several factors are considered and validated. For hearing, for example, we recognize timbre, intonation, acuity, orientation, personality, as well as the correspondence of the meaning of words/phrases used according to knowledge, grammars, lexicons, traditions, conventions, etc.

The lack of knowledge and effective intelligence, in today's information-processing artificial intelligence, is responsible in limiting authentication, which could do a lot better if it only knew.

© 2023 Consonance Publishing

5.5.2 Classification

Whereas authentication confirms participant qualification (authorization), classification qualifies data. This means that, in operation, both data and participants must be dynamically qualified, to enable the required security.

Other security management steps further consider the interaction between the two resource types: data and stakeholders.

Dynamic classification is the cornerstone of content-sharing security, enabling each piece of data to be valued and qualified according to its nature, purpose and operation.

Its operation is defined by the query context which includes the query's parameters, request sources, required and associated resources, qualified relationships that link and animate them, the desired use and more.

Based on the management of qualified relationships, dynamic classification is integrated into the very heart of each resource and relationship.

It is in operation, for each request and resource involved, that the processor evaluates dynamic classification and ensures access control by dynamically cross-referencing and correlating the three logical networks of:

Autorization	Classification	Context
Participants' rights and responsibilities network	Resources and their classification network	Context and applicable conditions network

For example, in *section 3 Key*, the vehicle, the intended object of sharing, carries its own value (replacement cost), but also that of the damage it may cause, the health of passengers, etc.

In this example, the insurers of those responsible, share the risk and bear witness to the classification of shared resources. It seems that when the risk is instantiated, the insurers will evaluate the exact classification in the context. Effective classification is dynamic.

Today, in information processing, data classification is still rare, always static, summary, intended for humans and restricted to a few arbitrary access profiles (restricted granularity), such as :

Typical Static Classification				
Top Secret	Secret	Confidential	Private	Public

Reality is too complex & evolving to be constrained to so little & so static.

© 2023 Consonance Publishing

5.5.3 CONTEXT

Context is an important factor to understand and manage. Inclusive, in addition to the request it includes what is related, such as: resources, their qualified relationships, applicable conditions, concurrent processes.

Context can also include reference to internal processes for analyzing, monitoring and adjusting (weighting, prioritizing) contexts to moderate biases that could affect the success of sharing, including unwanted interventions, for example.

THE KNOWLEDGE SHARING CONTEXT INCLUDES:

- The request, with its history and properties, including
  - Requester profiles and authorizations
  - Directly or indirectly targeted resources and relationships
  - Targeted operation types
  - Spatial and temporal localizations
  - Associated agreement
- Encoding, conversion, encryption aspects and constraints
- Noise, interference, and error
- Media used, and their constraints
- Validation of: accesses, applicable rules and conditions, statuses and others, without granularity limitations

Context analysis and management play a key role in access management, which combines the logical networks of classification, context and authorizations to evaluate each resource's sharing constraints, in the given context. They also contribute to the processing of external and metabolic streams.

With its arbitrary processing model, and no structured management of qualified relationships, information processing does not have access to the coherence of the natural knowledge processing model, optimized over the course of evolution and therefore significantly more mature.

 © 2023 Consonance Publishing

5.5.4 Entitlement

Typically, information processing defines certain access profiles, each associated with a set of rights and responsibilities, and where each participant is assigned to one of these profiles. Knowledge processing enables every knowledge resource to dynamically manage entitlement.

Each resource thus has its own evolving access profile, with its network of rights and responsibilities associated with the qualified relationships to which it contributes, according to each role it assumes for each of them.

Stakeholders, humans and systems, are also knowledge resources, and their rights and responsibilities are defined by each role they assume in each of their qualified relationship. Everything is dynamic, including management and governance. At any time and according to contexts, each resource can delegate functions for those delegated it.

Integrated into the qualified relationship management of every resource, in knowledge processing rights management is dynamic, contextual, and with a granularity only restricted by the structure of the considered reality.

For humans, managing rights and privileges is naturally rather intuitive and subconscious. It's even interesting to note the extent to which, intuitively, humans can effectively evaluate and weigh up a large number of interrelated factors, reflexes and algorithms.

For intelligent systems, qualified relationship management integration is also required.

5.5.5 Access

Access control is a critical and indispensable sharing & collaboration process.

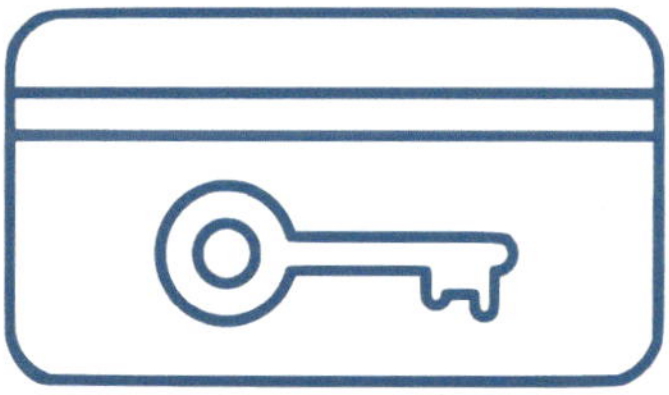

In principle, for each request, for each type of sharing required, for each resource to be shared, the processor evaluates the intersection and correlation of three main graphs[xiv] :

Data	Rights	Contexts
Targeted resources with qualified relationships	Rights, responsibilities, roles, authorizations	Contexts, requests, rules, conditions

Especially under high request volumes, performance of complex "real-time" process such as access control requires seriously optimized design.

© 2023 Consonance Publishing

5.5.6 Cryptography

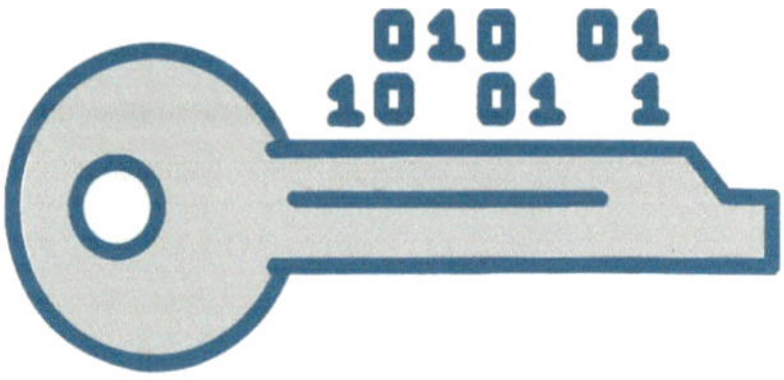

The main approach to protecting data and content, encryption requires the management of encryption keys that are essential for protecting and accessing data.

The complexity of managing encryption, its keys and their secure sharing can grow rapidly, especially with the proliferation of keys.

At its simplest, a key is required to encrypt and decrypt data. When data is shared with multiple "recipients," a "public" key can also be shared, while the sender of the data will own a private key.

Encryption keys must also be shared, and this sharing is typically secured by sharing other keys.

Data in transit is also typically encrypted systematically, resulting in additional levels of encryption where the same data is double-encrypted and decrypted. In fact, several encryption levels may be required, each with its own corresponding key management.

When the data is complex, it can be encrypted in several sections, each with its own keys and access levels.

In all case, the effective use of encryption keys is related to the access rights and contexts of the parties involved.

In addition, security and technology require regular replacement of keys.

There are many potential and typically evolving cases, each with its own layer of complexity. Hence, it quickly becomes clear that effective management of encryption and its keys requires intelligence, knowledge, and systematic management of the qualified relationships that organize resource networks.

5.5.7 Poisoning

Controlled data poisoning can be a useful tool to protect against duplication, AI imitation, or data scraping, for example, without compromising the value of the content.

Poisoning makes content readable, but inaccessible under certain conditions, such as replication, for example.

© 2023 Consonance Publishing

5.5.8 MONITORING

Each sharing defines its own conditions, often through the terms and appendices of collaboration agreement.

Essential to effective sharing, monitoring contributes to ensuring that each sharing complies with with the conditions of the applicable agreements.

The required follow-up and monitoring is typically part of the conditions. Its sophistication is often proportional to the value of the content shared.

Ensuring proper monitoring and follow-up can involve different elements and strategies, including :

5.5.8.1 IDENTIFICATION

Tracking shared resources first requires specific identification of resources. Identification is a prerequisite for management and for tracking.

For example in *section 3 Key*, the shared resource could be identified by combining the date/period, the vehicle registration certificate and the driver's license.

First qualification form, fundamental for any resource, a foundation of intelligence and knowledge, taking a multitude of forms, identification is addressed more specifically in *section 6 Artificial*.

5.5.8.2 TRACKING

Tracking operates at different levels, aiming to track the temporal, spatial and virtual location of shared resources, through their respective life cycles, according to agreement requirements and terms.

Tracking can combines different levels and types of processes, such as :

- **History** : Operation logging, chronology, Blockchains
- **Registration**: product guarantees, subscriptions
- **Tracing**: RF-ID, labeling
- **Steganography**[xv]: Imperceptible marking
- **Telemetry**: GPS, cameras, drones

In *section 3 Key*, the agreement is amicable, tracking could include, for example, vehicle ID, GPS transmitter, marked windows.

All approaches are valid, but their actual use relies on numerous factors assessed through the qualified relationships that structure resource networks.

5.5.9 COMPENSATION

Depending on the choice of the parties to the agreement, each transaction in a sharing arrangement can typically be associated with some compensation.

Compensation combines, systematizes and automates :

- The many diverse compensation modes, including:
  - Traditional transactional modes
  - Automated modes, such as :
    - Usage-based invoicing, rather than purchase or rental
    - Micro-payment, as with pay-per-use billing, for example
- Monitoring, distribution and updating agreements.

Compensation can take the form of fees, recurring or non-recurring, or, as in *section 3 Key*, without formal compensation, but with a few good bottles of wine brought back, for example.

Managing collaboration and sharing security includes distributing compensations, with precision, efficiency, validation and according to the different modes, stages, and monitoring, in compliance with applicable agreements.

THE MEETING OF TWO PERSONALITIES IS LIKE THE CONTACT OF TWO CHEMICAL SUBSTANCES: IF THERE IS ANY REACTION, BOTH ARE TRANSFORMED

CARL GUSTAV JUNG

THERE ARE AS MANY MOLECULES IN A DROP OF WATER AS STARS IN THE KNOWN UNIVERSE: 10000 BILLION BILLION (10^{22})

© 2023 Consonance Publishing

© 2023 Consonance Publishing

6 Artificial

Following on from concepts related to causes and foundations, in the previous sections, this section considers some concepts related to the approach to computerizing (artificial) knowledge and intelligence.

The dual objective is to
1. To enable intelligent systems to process knowledge with intelligence, as humans naturally do
2. To ensure that collaboration between humans and intelligent systems is deep, meaningful, long-lasting, productive and adequately framed.

As the fruit and tools of evolution, humans contribute to evolution. They develop intelligent systems to work and live with them, collaborating to optimize productivity, prosperity and solidarity. As first priority, intelligent systems are called upon to support three forms of collaboration:

humans	humans + systems	systems
Where systems contribute by supporting and securing collaboration between humans	Where, the more compatible & closer systems are to natural human experience, the more relevant and effective sharing and collaboration, can be	Where compatibility is essential and ensured through the specification of international knowledge representation and sharing standards and rules

In today's massive AI context, systems offer and use arbitrary services through APIs, invoking corresponding server functions. Better than before, it remains "manually assembled", on a client/server foundation, with massive aging and brittle assets, that need to be evolved and accelerated, in performance, diversity, complexity and agility. Energy and water (cooling) are already astronomical.

**ARTIFICIAL KNOWLEDGE & INTELLIGENCE
ENABLE BETTER EVOLVING RESOURCES, ABILITIES, COLLABORATIVE PRODUCTIVITY, PROSPERITY & SOLIDARITY**

Knowledge processing is organized and articulated, especially around:
- Natural and proven knowledge-processing models
- Continuous metabolic processes optimizing & evolving knowledge-backgrounds
- Continuous parallel sensory & motor stream processing
- Knowledge resource modeling and representation
- Qualified relationship modeling and management
- Efficient use and management of archetypes and metadata
- Logical operational structures: resources, relationships, graphs/networks

© 2023 Consonance Publishing

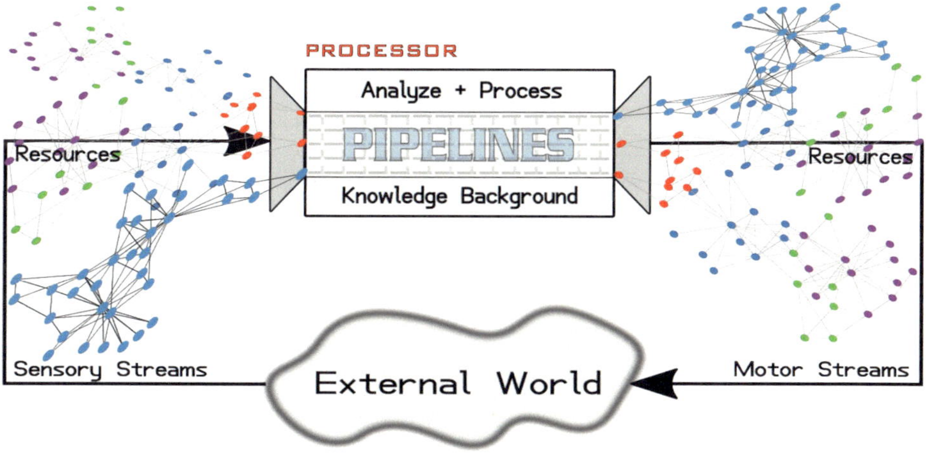

6.1 MODEL

The knowledge processing model is designed:

- According to the natural model, at human scale
- Around human or system knowledge processors, where each :
    - Evolves its knowledge background over :
        - Interactions with the outside world, by processing input sensory (inference) and output motor (projection) streams
        - Internal continuous processes of knowledge metabolism that evaluate, qualify, correlate and evolve knowledge resources
    - Is motivated to collaborate to evolution

See also *section 9.2.1 Nature*.

The processing of sensor (input) and motor (output) streams uses parallel[xvi] transformation pipelines and is always operated relatively to the processor's knowledge-background.

Interaction contributes to the processor's knowledge-background & metabolism.

The knowledge-background represents the sum of the processor's knowledge. It also serves as its reference base. Some of this knowledge is inherited (DNA, common core), while the rest is acquired or deduced/inferred through interaction.

Collaboration enables each processor to interact, operate, monitor, qualify its interaction with others as well as their reaction to its own contribution, in feedback loops, optimizing its knowledge-background, evolving it.

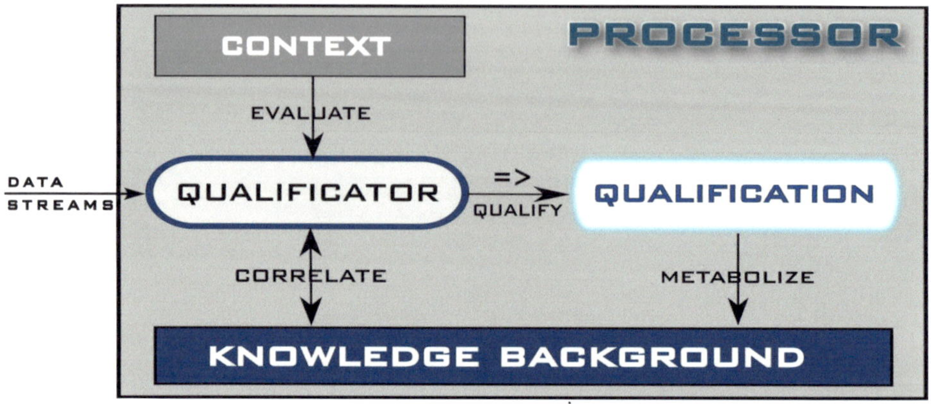

6.1.1 Qualification

The mind is relative and relativistic. Basically, it analyzes, compares, evaluates, orients and integrates. In short, it qualifies.

Fundamental to knowledge as well as to its operation and sharing, qualification relativizes a resource by evaluating it in its specific context and comparing and correlating this with the processor's current knowledge-background, known resources. The result of the qualification operation is also a qualification.

Qualification takes an infinite variety of forms, including, among the simplest and most basic: identification, classification, as well as temporal, spacial and electronic location.

Performance indicators (KPIs) are examples of calculated qualifications. Even in natural languages, verbs, nouns, adjectives are qualification forms, as:

Item	Qualify & Identify	Target
Substantive (Noun)	=>	Entity
Adjective	=>	Substantive
Verb	=>	Behavior, Action

Knowledge and intelligence are built on qualification.

Of all the forms of qualification, the first, and indispensable to the existence of each resource, is identification. See *section 6.2 Archetypes*.

Each resource is a collection of qualification, at its level, and a qualification for the resources to which it contributes.

 © 2023 Consonance Publishing

6.1.2 Resource

Vast and diversified, like the structure of the reality that it represents, knowledge logically organizes around qualification, and through qualification collections, operating in logical networks (graphs), where:

A) Resources are knowledge's building blocks

B) A knowledge resource is an identified collection of qualifications

C) A collection of resources is a resource

D) Qualified relationships between resources are resources

E) Qualified relationships define and structure (qualify) resource collaboration

F) Qualified relationships articulate knowledge-resource graphs

G) Knowledge-resource graphs are knowledge resources

H) Knowledge comprises all identifiable knowledge-resource networks

I) Knowledge only includes identified or identifiable knowledge-resources

J) Resources have types and archetypes

K) Identification the first qualification form, frames every resource's existence, as only the identifiable can be referenced and managed

L) Identification can take many forms

ISBN# 978-1-7389132-1-3

Section 6.2 Archetypes considers some basic archetypes of which the identified resource is the root. *Section 6.2.2 Relationship* more specifically considers qualified relationships.

6.2 ARCHETYPES

Processing knowledge also processes meta-knowledge, "knowledge about knowledge". Computerized meta-knowledge becomes knowledge metadata. Meta-knowledge is multi-layered.

Essential for knowledge processing, particularly for modeling and managing resource streams processing, meta-knowledge takes advantage of the natural archetype model, which enables the management of :

- Resource types and models, qualifying their nature, structure, operation
- Archetypes themselves
- Common parameters and attributes for different resource types/families
- Qualifications, defined, inherited or acquired, for each resource

Both for external streams resource processing and for metabolism processes, both for qualified relationships and for other resources (entities), meta-knowledge is organized in evolving layers, continuously correlated and optimized, by the processor's metabolism processing.

Meta-knowledge is foundational to knowledge and consciousness (metacognition).

ARCHETYPES ARE LIKE RIVERBEDS
WHICH DRY UP WHEN THE WATER DESERTS THEM,
BUT WHICH IT CAN FIND AGAIN AT ANY TIME

CARL GUSTAV JUNG

Archetypes are knowledge resources that constitute meta-knowledge structures and are typically used as models and templates, in qualifying structural and operational resource characteristics.

Archetypes :

- Are themselves derived from other archetypes
- Structure resource matching, analysis and processing
- Guide resource interpretation and behavior
- Enable defining, adapting and structuring based on associated archetypes
- Enable managing resource participation to qualified relationships
- Manage and contribute to resource metadata

The "vehicle" archetype, for example, qualifies what is common to the various types of vehicle.

The "vehicle" archetype, for example, qualifies what is common to all vehicles. It is graph resource used to define different types or families od vehicles like motorcycle, bicycle, car, bus, truck, etc..

 © 2023 Consonance Publishing

Resources refer to archetypes, and modifying an archetype, from then on modifies the structure and operation of the resources that refer to it.

Some common archetypes are introduced further below, like: identification, location, role, application.

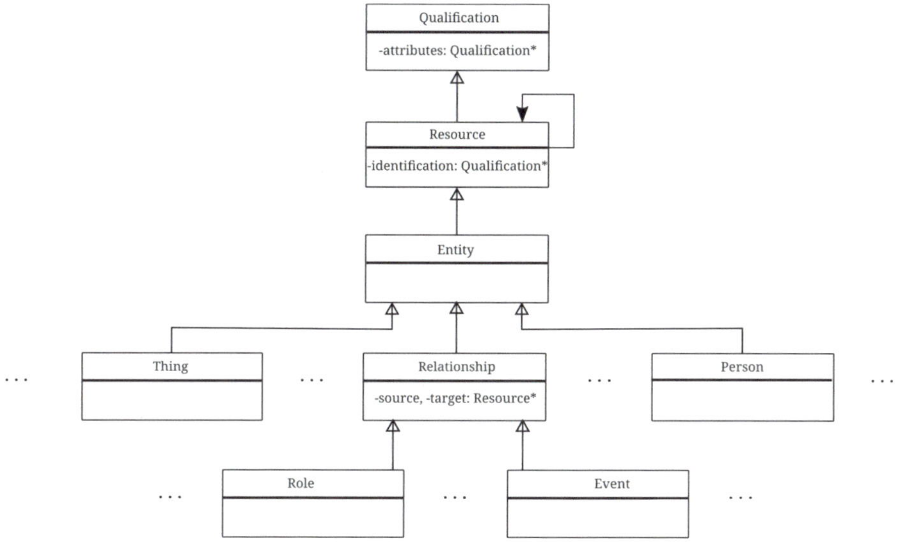

The UML-style diagram above, presents the initial archetype hierarchy levels, from which all others inherit:

- Resources (Qualification collections)
- Entities, from which all resources derive, directly or indirectly
- Qualified Relationships, structuring knowledge and from which all qualified relationships derive, directly or indirectly
- Other archetypes

6.2.1 Entity

In the context here, "entities" refer to resources that do not define a qualified relationship between other resources.

Like the leaves of a tree, at the end of branch networks, entities are the resources at the end of relationship networks, the leaves. Entities designate the non-relational aspects of the structure of reality. See also Relationship below.

Entity types are unlimited and often include objects, places, concepts, physical or virtual, for example.

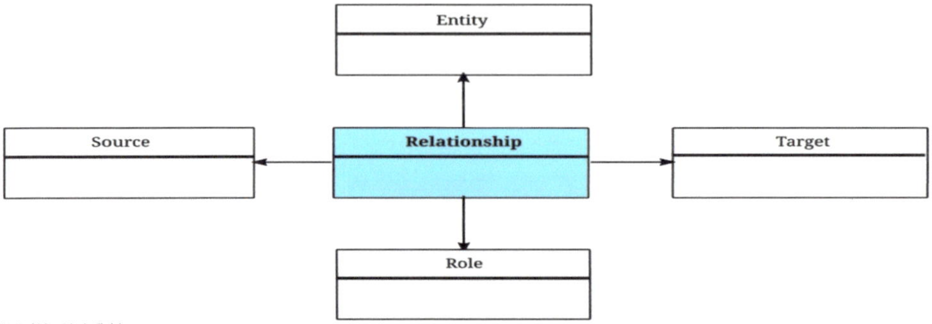

6.2.2 Relationship

Qualified relationships are resources, like others, except that they also qualify, model, manage and operate relationships between other resources.

Each qualified relationship specifies the characteristics of the relationship (specification), the terms of the tacit or explicit agreement, as well as the roles & behaviors of its source and target, in the relationship context.

Rooted in the relativity and transformation of existence, qualified relationship management is a foundation of thought, intelligence and knowledge.

Although entities are numerous and diverse, relationships are typically much more so, since their sources and targets are not limited to entities alone, as they also apply to any source and target resources, of any kind, including relationships, at any level. Qualified relationships between qualified relationships are common.

Qualified relationships are structuring and strategic. They are determining for knowledge and intelligence, both natural and artificial.

Basically, every relationship is directional, between its source and target. Multidirectional relationships are collections of relationships. As well, relationship targets and sources can be complex resources, such as groups, lists, or collections, for example.

Each relationship defines, motivates and frames the actions and behaviors of its source and target. Qualified relationships implement the agreement between the respective parties, as well as frame their contributions.

Qualified relationships structure knowledge and its processing. Information processing prioritizes entities, underestimating relationships and typically reducing them to simple references, without fully understanding and modeling them and without enabling systems to effectively manage them (metabolism).

 © 2023 Consonance Publishing

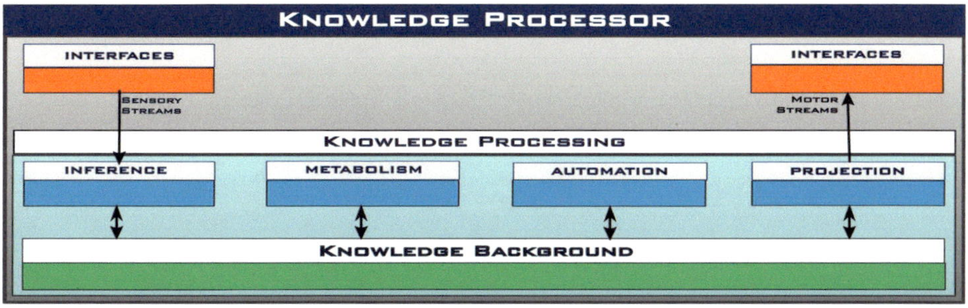

6.2.3 Processor

The processor is the central archetype of the knowledge-processing architecture model. Resources of this archetype, such as humans and effectively intelligent systems, can process and share knowledge resources.

The diagram above highlights aspects of the relationship between the processor's knowledge-background and the associated metabolic integration processes. Blue indicates operating components (code), green indicates knowledge banks (data), and orange is reserved for external streams. Each processor has at least all these components:

Background	Combines inherited and acquired knowledge
Metabolism	Continuous knowledge-background optimizing/evolving processes
Intelligence	Knowledge processing ability
Automation	Reflexes, habits, conditioning, triggering, automation
Interaction	Ability to continuously process sensory and motor streams
Interface	Secure modular human-system interfaces
Integration	Modular integration of external streams (infer, project)

Human processors operate intuitively, but artificial processors depend on humans to know intuition.

6.2.3.1 Background

The processor's knowledge-background is his reference base in everything. A large proportion of the processor's resources are invested in maintaining, growing, optimizing and evolving its background, especially through its metabolic processes. See Metabolism.

6.2.3.2 Automation

Reflexes and automation enable the processor to record and automate potentially complex behavior sequences, to the deep or subconscious mind, freeing the conscious mind from having to manage recurring execution details.

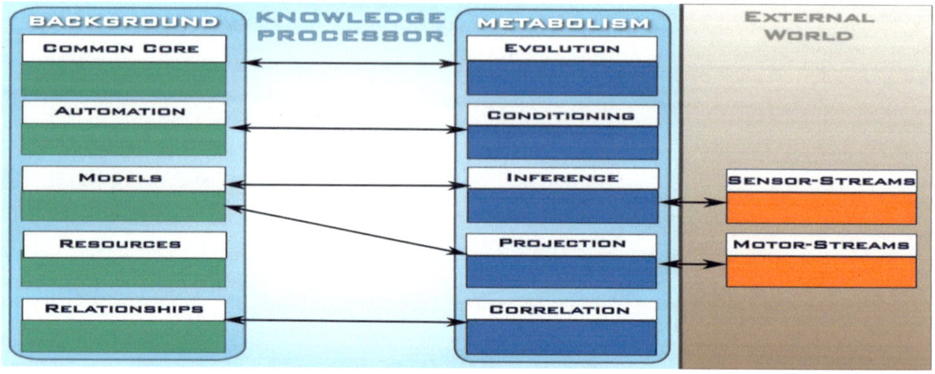

6.2.3.3 METABOLISM

Each processor's metabolism refers to its continuous knowledge-background evolution processes, including integration, correlation, and optimization.

CONTINUOUS KNOWLEDGE-BACKGROUND EVOLUTION

All processing is carried out and integrated relative to the processor's current knowledge-background. This background, all its knowledge, is fundamental to its operation. Each processor can integrate into its knowledge-background, resources deduced or inferred from its interactions (sensory and motor streams) or through its metabolic processes.

From the intention of integrating it, and for the rest of its existence in the processor's background, each resource is subject to metabolic processes.

Operating continuously, at full throttle during sleep and in the background when awake, metabolic functions evolve the processor's knowledge background.

INFER	QUALIFY	INTEGRATE	CORRELATE	PROJECT

Metabolism optimizes and evolves all knowledge-background resources, correlating, optimizing and evolving them, starting from qualified relationships.

Through metabolic processes, integrated resources are progressively metabolized, further consolidated, integrated, correlated, ever more deeply into the processor's knowledge background.

Metabolic processes also include predictive functions that enables event or behavior anticipation based on the history of available resources (experience).

Reflexes, habits and automation are subject to metabolic knowledge processing, for maintenance, optimization and evolution. See *section 4.5.6 Reflexes*.

© 2023 Consonance Publishing

6.2.4 Role

Key to every qualified relationship, itself a relation in a relation, The Role archetype qualifies the responsibility of a resource for a task.

Roles are typically used to specify potential or required responsibilities and behaviors for the source and target of each qualified relationship.

6.2.5 Location

Location is relatively fundamental archetype that enables locating a resource in physical or electronic space. Combining position and period, in practice, location is associated with some serious challenges especially given the multitude of common and often misaligned and redundant references, axes, conventions, and formats.

Locating resources is indispensable and operates along three main axes:

Temporal	Period, duration, repetition, date, time
Geo-spatial	Position, address, 2D, 3D, XD, code, etc.
Electronic	URL/URI, email, phone, etc.

Location is multidimensional, and often redundant, combining:

- References along the three main axis
- Various channels on each axis
- Different forms and variants for every channel

6.2.5.1 Position

Position enables locating resources in physical and electronic spaces. Typically combines various location forms, from a large variety.

Locating and airport, for example, could combine airport, maritime, railroad codes, postal codes, regional civic addresses, 2D or 3D coordinate sets (longitude, latitude, altitude), geometric sets (points, areas, volumes), electronic addresses, including phones, radios, email, messaging, fax, URLs and others, each evolving in time, at its own rhythm.

6.2.5.2 Period

Archetype of temporal location, "period" includes date, time, duration, periodicity, frequencies. It also qualifies evolution life cycles, change, log, behavior, synchronization, sequencing, etc.

Period is used to index causality and its management is key to intelligence and knowledge processing.

© 2023 Consonance Publishing

6.2.6 Application

Application is the archetype of executable resources. This archetype supports all application types and forms including source & object code. Like all resources, applications can be assembled and nested (graphs).

In the context of the operation of a knowledge processor, the applications considered here can be found at three main levels:

- **Interaction**: processing of sensory and motor streams, along pipelines
- **Evolution**: metabolic processes for optimizing knowledge background
- **Conditioning**: management of reflexes, habits, automation

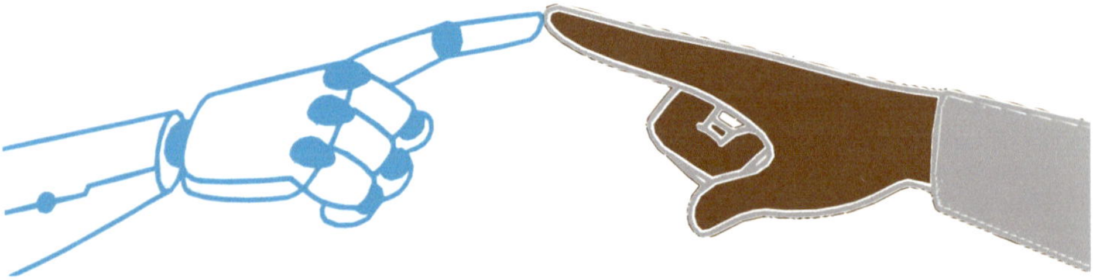

6.2.7 Interface

The Interface archetype is a specialization of the application archetype, designed to manage the processor's interaction with the outside world.

Dealing with sensory and motor streams, through adapted input and output content-handlers, where, for example, a speech interface could combine speech synthesis and recognition, two very different operations, each with its own specific content-handler(s).

Interfaces can use more than one or two content-handlers, as interactive virtual reality interfaces may use many concurrent input and output streams.

Processing knowledge enables the development of interfaces between humans and intelligent systems, as well as between intelligent systems.

 © 2023 Consonance Publishing

6.3 Data

Data is the computer representation of content.

In information processing, content is strictly informational.

With knowledge-resources and qualified-relationships modeling and management, with sensory and motor stream processing, knowledge processing allows knowledge-processors to share knowledge-resources either directly as knowledge data, or as informational views and artifacts, through projection and inference and through their interfaces and content managers operating informational codifications.

In addition to effectively representing knowledge-resources, as well as their graphs and structures, the representation of knowledge data is optimized according to key aspects of the operational context:

- **Secure**: Integrating security aspects, see *section 5.5 Security*
- **Generic**[xvii]: Generalizing and optimizing content processing
- **Streaming**: Congruence between streaming, parallelism and transformation pipeline processing

6.3.1 Stream

The natural model's processing mode, processing parallel streams at input (sensory), internally (metabolic), and at output (motor), offers several significant advantages, such as:

- Common processing mode on input, internally, and on output
- Data is processed without latency, without having to wait for stream end
- Stream latency frees resources for other processing
- Important flexibility and performance gains, accentuated by volume
- Pattern recognition (data/metadata) activated processing

6.3.2 Pipeline

External and internal knowledge-resource streams cross parallel transformation-pipeline networks, in each processor's mind, where the processes and applications that detect, analyze, select, transform and route data, are installed.

Dynamic metadata management guides routing and processing, enabling resource matching and applicability based on their respective nature and structure.

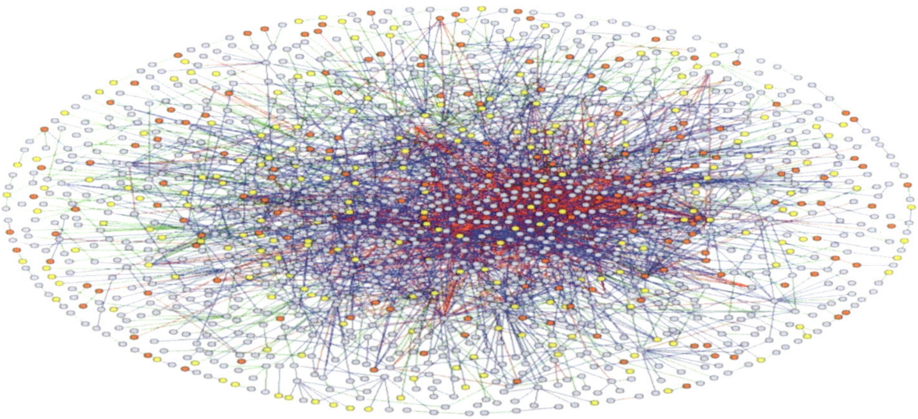

6.3.3 Correlation

Correlation is a form of qualification based on evaluating common and complementary factors between resources, as well as formalizing the matches, for subsequent reference and use. The formalization process typically results in the creation resources in processor knowledge-backgrounds.

Qualified relationships are key to correlation, since they define and qualify resources, relationships, responsibilities and behaviors.

The metabolic correlation process, is fundamental to knowledge & intelligence operation. Many thought processes rely on correlation, like stream processing, metabolism, reflexes, judgment, tolerance, prioritization, security, etc.

 © 2023 Consonance Publishing

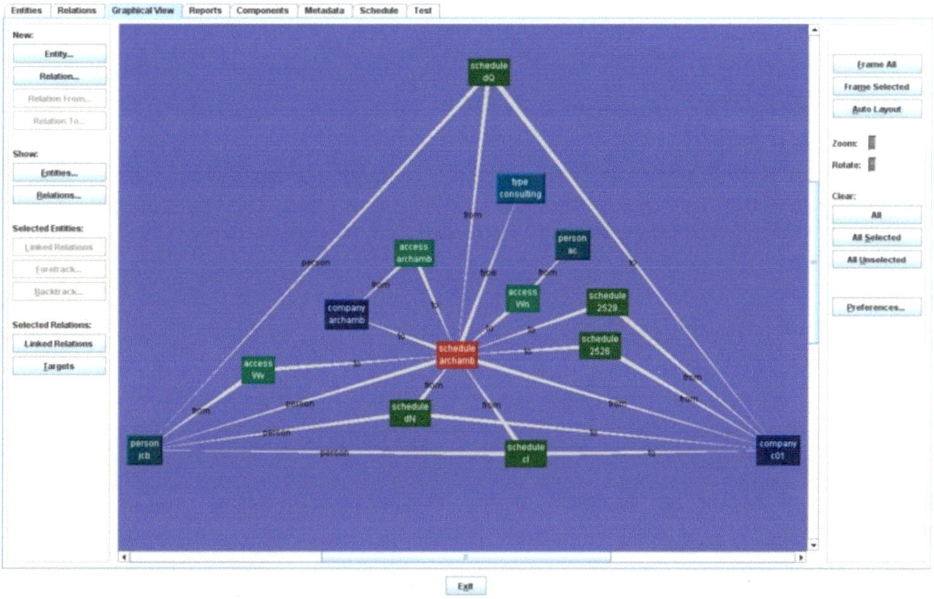

6.3.4 Graph

At the boundary between the abstract and the concrete, between a concept and its projection into reality, graphs are ideal natural structures for representing and managing the knowledge's richness and sophistication, since:

- Qualified relationships, a major knowledge foundation, naturally structure resources into logical networks
- Graphs are the logical, electronic, and physical network model
- A resource graph is a resource, with no nesting limits
- Graphs are the most flexible and generic data structure for modeling and managing all data types, especially for knowledge data and metadata
- Graphs are the most comprehensive and processable data structure
- The numerous graph processing algorithms and techniques are well proven, cataloged, and documented
- Many tools are available for analyzing, processing, and visualizing graphs
- Optimized graph processing offers optimal performance that is typically unmatched

IMPACTS

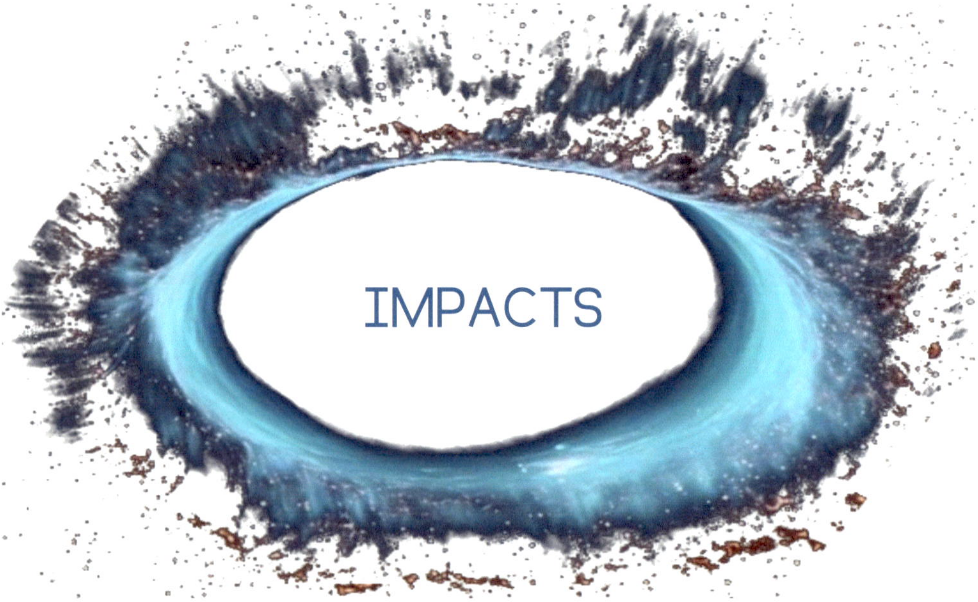

© 2023 Consonance Publishing

7 Impacts

Developing intelligent systems requires considering their impacts. In all causality and relativity, approaches, design, ethics, frameworks and consequences, for generations, need to be carefully considered.

Current AI has not yet fully considered most of these aspects. Not only is it unable to formulate a code of ethics or a regulatory approach, but its development is already serving to reduce human freedoms and place the destiny of humanity in the hands of a wealthy few, through digital identity, banking control, and social credit, for example.

The impacts of artificially processing knowledge are many and varied, but they can be grouped, as this section considers these impact types:

1. **Applicative**: impacts related to application development:
   - existing applications, new applications
2. **Collective**: societal impacts, or relating to the community, including :
   - ethics, nature, technology, economics, society, politics

7.1 Applicative

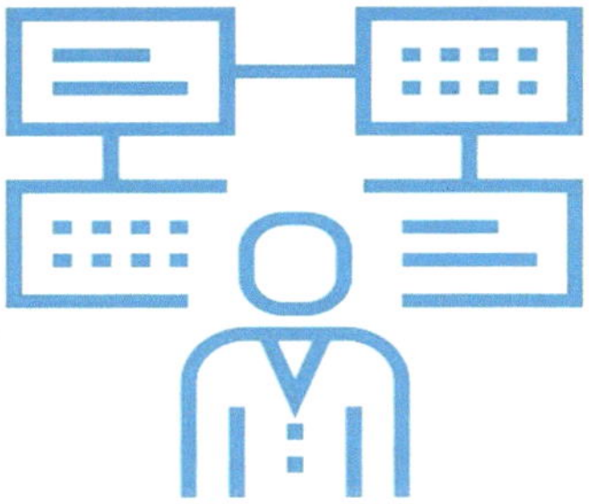

A few use cases can help better consider knowledge processing impacts on applications and application development .

This section groups these examples into two main types and sub-section:

1. **Existing**: Evolving existing application types
2. **New**: Developing emerging application types

7.1.1 Existing

To evolve existing application types, knowledge processing offers tools that enable better addressing certain common shortcomings that still plague today's IT environments, systems, applications, and developments.

These new tools include those related to qualification, security, governance, integration, consistency, and ontology, for example.

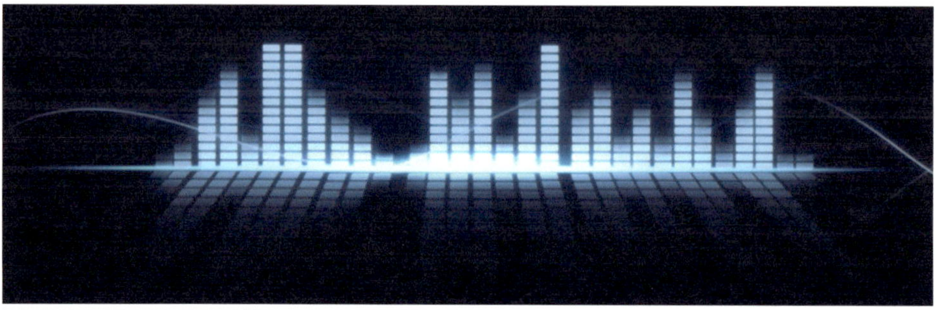

7.1.1.1 QUALIFICATION

Qualification is the fundamental operation of intelligence. All knowledge and intelligence operations are based on qualification.

Understanding qualification allows knowledge to be processed artificially.

The conscious and systematic use of qualification, through the management of qualified relationships, for example, provides better tools for complex dynamic context solutions, inaccessible to information processing.

Several important dynamic processes, such as those related to security (classification, rights, contexts), for example, are naturally structured around the management of qualified relationships and qualification.

Qualification, and especially qualified relationships management, from knowledge processing, can provide new tools and approaches for evolving many application types, for example, for:

- complexity management, judgment, tolerance
- solving recurring problems, such as those related to secure sharing

Systematic qualification management also makes it possible to evolve identification, evaluation, correlation, pattern recognition, classification, as well as governance and security management, all of which can impact the evolution of existing application types.

A fundamental operation of thought, qualification potentially impacts:

- All aspects of intelligence and knowledge processing
- All application types

The impacts of qualification and its systematic management are profound in that they affect approaches, but for many types of applications, this type of evolution opens the door to levels of productivity that are typically still unmatched or unattainable.

© 2023 Consonance Publishing

7.1.1.2 Security

Section 5.5 Security introduces security aspects that are essential to sharing and collaboration, fundamental activities of human intelligence and creativity.

Processing knowledge and managing qualified relationships makes it possible to better manage complexity.

Today, not only is complexity the enemy of security, undermining it, but the operation of security itself is highly complex. At every level, every day, complexity is accelerating its growth.

Today, we respond to security threats by adding tools and layers of tools, which accentuates this complexity and its management, further weakening environments.

Meanwhile, incidents, damage, victims, and defense and protection costs are increasing. Worse still, this context prevents a real knowledge economy from developing and bringing the prosperity necessary for the survival of the majority of humans. See *section 7.2.4.1 Reduction*.

The security industry is growing, but, still overwhelmed, it is turning to massive AI in an attempt to limit risks and freedoms.

This same massive AI is also replacing human labor in the industrial economy, leaving the majority of humans increasingly constrained, impoverished, deprived of hope, and threatened with extermination.

In fact, security, especially content, sharing and collaboration security, is essential to the survival of civilization, the human race, and the ecosystem. See *section 7.2.4 Economy*.

Knowledge processing, systematic modeling and management of qualified relationships, effective natural and artificial intelligence, and their collaboration are key to the future of humans.

The integration of knowledge processing into existing types of applications represents a step on the indispensable transition towards new generations of intelligent applications and processing. See *section 7.2.4.2 Transition*.

7.1.1.3 Governance

The governance of any resource combines monitoring and control of its operation to optimize and evolve its quality and performance

Operating continuously, governance is a metabolic process that ensures the quality, integrity, operation, evolution, and useful life of each resource, from the simplest to the most complex, such as, for example, multinational enterprises with divisions, groups, departments, processes, services, products, human and physical resources, systems, etc., according to associated indicators, thresholds, and reflexes.

The governance of each resource uses key performance indicators (KPIs), each with its thresholds, targets, effective values, tolerances, adjustment rules, priority constraints, and others, allowing the resource to dynamically evaluate, monitor, control, and adjust its operation and behavior, in its collaborations.

Intrinsic to knowledge, governance enables each resource to understand its operation in order to better evolve it.

Natural in knowledge processing, governance remains theoretical in information processing, where, at best, humans try to keep an eye on things, giving themselves guidelines and indicators that they manage essentially manually.

However, the number, complexity, and evolution of resources do not allow for effective governance without systematic management of qualified relationships integrating dynamic indicators, with proper adjustment and weighting mechanisms, under intelligent computer control.

Dynamic modeling and management of qualified relationships can enable existing application types to gradually approach systematic governance.

 © 2023 Consonance Publishing

7.1.1.4 INTEGRATION

Data integration is a key aspect and foundation, of both application and market integration.

Information and knowledge processing differ in their approach. Considering these differences shows the ways in which integration can have an impact:

7.1.1.4.1 INFORMATION

In today's organizations, each application determines the data and formats it uses, according to its various use cases.

Between application pair, transformations are installed, ETLs (Extract, Transform, Load) for example, i.e. a third-party application configured to adapt the data from the first application for the second.

In a large organization, for example, there may be hundreds of thousands of applications in use. Where is the enterprise data? What format is it in? When is it protected, and when is it less?

Worse still, everything changes continually and transformations must be adapted to every administrative, technical or software evolution.

Well-experienced humans are responsible for this manual, tailor-made work, and must, in principle, also keep the documentation up to date...

In such a context, integration presents a expensive perpetual challenge and a typically unattainable goal. In trying to compensate, many turn to data virtualization for:

- **Access**: a data virtualization application layer is added between the actual data and a view adapted to usage requirements
- **Model**: A master data model (MDM) aims to provide enterprise architects with a view of the organization's canonical data.

Many organizations use both. In both cases, laboriously developed, and, in principle constantly updated, each of these views :

- Adds a new application layer on top of the actual data
- Contributes to application, interface and transformation multiplication
- Squares overall complexity
- Systems, applications and data are not effectively integrated
- The view remains a snapshot of the data at one point in time
- Need to manage correspondence between the views and actual data
- Little integrating or structuring impact
- Detrimental to efficiency and governance

7.1.1.4.2 Knowledge

The processing model presented, with its resources, processors, backgrounds, archetypes, qualified relationships, metabolism, streams, reflexes, classification, qualification, processing pipelines, etc., reflects the natural model of knowledge evolved and structured by nature over billions of years.

Knowledge is the operational basis of everything, including humans. Its model is neither an accessory nor an option; it is the foundation.

Therefore, understanding it seems essential and full of strategic lessons. Without knowledge, and therefore without intelligence, nothing is possible. On the contrary, knowledge has made everything that exists possible and allows for much more. No human can invent any better, but with knowledge, anything becomes possible.

The proposed knowledge-processing aims to enable systems to collaborate intelligently with humans. The impacts of knowledge processing on systems and applications are paradigm-shifting.

The management of archetypes and its impact as the foundation of a natural and generic ontological structure, integrating, contextualizing, and qualifying the relationships, behaviors, and interactions between knowledge resources, offers infinite ramifications affecting the design and development of applications, whether they are common, emerging, or future application types.

Knowledge-processing affects value scales and priorities, while making possible what would not be otherwise.

All human activities and all existing application types can benefit from this in many ways.

KNOWLEDGE CREATES AND USES INFORMATION ALSO PROVIDING ITS MEANING

© 2023 Consonance Publishing

7.1.1.5 Coherence

Through the continuous metabolism of their knowledge background, knowledge-processors ensure coherence and consistency[xviii] of data, processes, and systems.

Essential to effective communication and decision-making, coherence and consistency contribute to data and systems clarity, credibility, and reliability.

Responsible for ensuring coherence and consistency in their knowledge-background, knowledge-processors must therefore:

- Manage archetypes and metadata
- Ensure dynamic governance
- Log all operations
- Validate, correlate, and optimize resources
- Ensure the integrity of data and operations
- Manage, monitor and evolve qualified relationships
- Replace redundancy and duplication with references
- Ensure extensive management of transactional contexts
- Validate the structure of the model and its integration processes
- Integrate security and dynamic classification at the heart of resources
- Ensure unlimited granularity of data, contexts, and processing
- Ensure systematic external stream processing
- Control structured and secure access to data and resources

On the other hand, information processing increases complexity and the risk of inconsistency by multiplying silos, data, formats, transformations, and redundancies, while coherence, integration, and governance remain manually and arbitrarily ensured by humans.

The less controlled complexity of environments and systems confronts them with significant challenges in terms of coherence and consistency, which are especially critical for data, like trying to search for the "authoritative source" of data from an application instance, for example.

Coherent and consistent knowledge processing offers significant advantages for evolving existing application types.

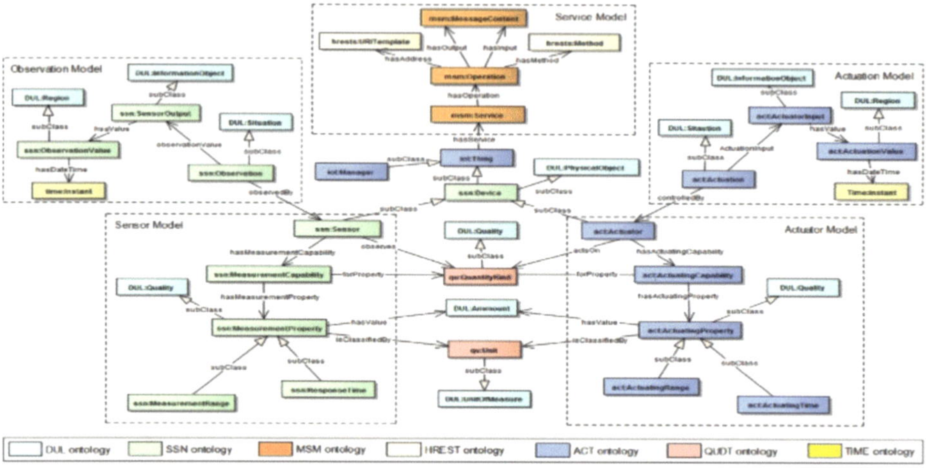

7.1.1.6 ONTOLOGY

Ontology aims at identifying and correlating reality structures, their relationships, organization, networks and hierarchies.

For knowledge processing, ontology is trying to define resources, relationships and archetypes that structure knowledge.

As intelligence is the ability to process knowledge and relies on the identification of its resources, ontology tries to identify what intelligence processes. The complementarity seems notable.

Today, the difference stems mostly from the fact that knowledge processing requires anchoring to nature and the underlying natural phenomena, while current ontological development efforts often seem arbitrary, lacking sound integration and grounding in knowledge architecture. It remains arbitrarily anchored to varied committee tentative consensus. Too prone to human biases, as result, ontology compatibility still pose major challenges.

Nature has developed an excellent model which, if properly understood, provides required foundations to better anchor ontology.

Ontology is naturally intuitive and subconscious. Everyone knows the difference and the (qualified) relationships between the chair and the table, for example. On the other hand, for intelligent systems, moving from dream to reality, at this point, requires being much more specific.

Integrating ontology and knowledge-processing development efforts can provide mutual light and enable optimizing learning and knowledge management.

 © 2023 Consonance Publishing

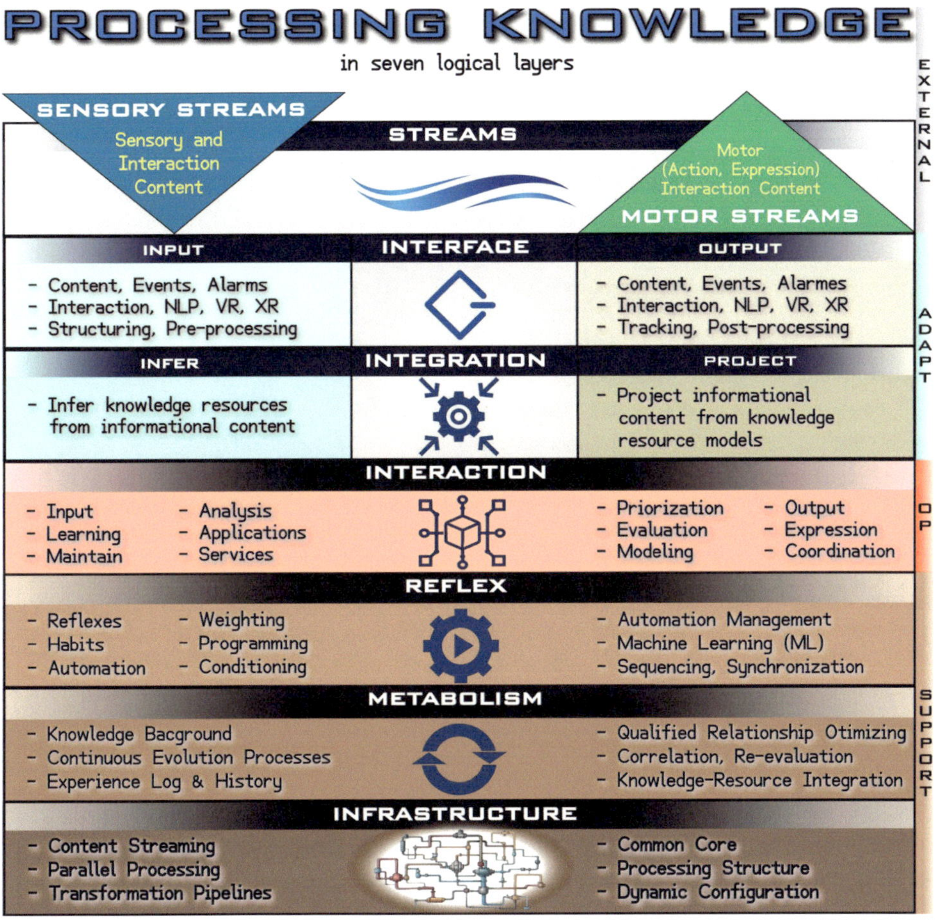

7.1.2 New

Processing knowledge enables the development of new solutions :

- For existing application problems
- Addressing new application problem types:
  - Integrating emerging technology approaches with knowledge processing
  - Inaccessible to information processing

This section introduces a few examples and considerations on:

1. ML: Machine Learning	4. Robotics
2. NLP/LLM: Natural Language Processing	5. Collaboration
3. VR: Virtual/Mix Reality (XR)	6. Infrastructure

7.1.2.1 ML

Machine learning (ML), a major segment of today's AI, is an interesting approach where large-scale computing systems analyze massive amounts of specialized information, under human supervision and training, to develop sophisticated automated responses.

Tesla's autonomous driver (FSD), analyzed more than 3 billion kilometers of road driving video, as well as consented data from millions of vehicles on the road, to learn how to drive.

The results are impressive, FSD is downloadable to vehicles, and statistically causes fewer accidents and less damage than human drivers.

This interesting and innovative project, is not within everyone's budget. Already estimated at hundreds of billions of dollars, the project could reach a trillion. Clearly this AI is massive, as is also its water and electricity consumption.

Machine learning allows the system to sort certain forms of information in a potentially refined and efficient manner. However, the system has no intelligence or reason, other than seemingly, and it is prone to human bias.

In knowledge processing, ML, as well as some ML functions can potentially be integrated in different artificial knowledge-processor operations, especially around those related to reflex and automation conditioning, for example.

Knowledge processing can also contribute to enriching machine learning applications, such as from: framing, semantics, granularity, judgment, self-correction, and metabolism, for example.

The average AI error rate remains relatively high, at around 15% under good conditions. Each answer has a margin of error that can only be detected by those who know the correct answer, but in this case, the usefulness of AI is questionable.

Should this AI be managing human activities?

 © 2023 Consonance Publishing

7.1.2.2 NLP

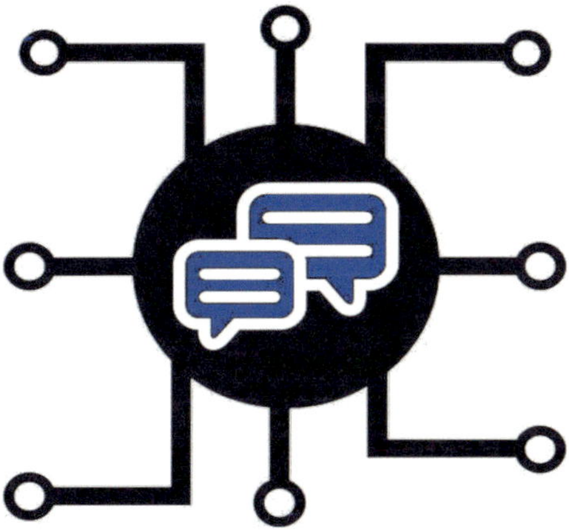

Natural language processing (NLP) and machine learning (ML) are pillars of today's AI. Large language models (LLMs) and generative AI add successive specialization layers.

While machine learning aims to enable systems to learn, NLPs (LLMs, Gen AI) focus on interpreting human natural languages.

The most popular AIs today include Grok, Claude, and ChatGPT.

Natural languages are natural because they are intuitive and subconscious. As such, they play an important role in human verbal and written communication.

Developed from conventions and long traditions, they are complex, relatively arbitrary tools, shaped by usage and built on prerequisite knowledge.

Natural language processing (NLP) aims primarily to enable systems to communicate more directly with humans.

These applications also serve translation, document analysis and correction, as well as providing writing assistance.

To knowledge processing, natural language processing (NLP) provides valuable or strategic interfaces.

The LLMs and generative AI approach is based on statistical prediction of the "next word".

Alternately, knowledge processing allows for the use of more meaningful and nuanced content, not limited to a portion of the information available on the Internet, but also, and perhaps more importantly, based on the experience and knowledge-background of each processor, as well as on the evaluation and processing of qualified-relationship networks.

THE DESCRIPTION IS NOT THE DESCRIBED

JIDDU KRISHNAMURTI

7.1.2.3 Virtual Reality

Like natural language processing, virtual reality offers intelligent systems, better human adapted multimedia communication interface foundations.

THE EXPRESSION VIRTUAL REALITY INCLUDES HERE VARIOUS FORMS		
VR	**Virtual reality**	Multimedia representation of synthesized reality
AR	**Augmented reality**	Adds virtual elements to physical reality
XR	**Mixed Reality**	Combines virtual, physical and augmented reality

Today, virtual reality applications can mostly be found in :

- Games and entertainment, such as in World of Warcraft
- Industrial, medical and military applications:
    - Drones and remote-controlled or autonomous vehicles
    - Visualization and control
    - Simulation and training
- Virtual reality social networks such as SecondLife

Virtual reality support technology has been developing for several decades already. The SecondLife social network has been operating (evolving) an interactive 3D universe online, with millions of users, since 1986.

Virtual reality technology continues to evolve. However, virtual reality applications remain relatively marginal and marked by significant business failures, such as Meta's Meta-verse.

These failures or delays seem to be related to:

- **Security**: Lack of functionality due to inadequate sharing security
- **Matrialism**: Investments in tools more than content
- **Intelligence**: attractive facade, but lacking in system intelligence
- **Creativity**: Limited by preceding points and ill-adapted social constraints

Markets, products, and services supported by a secure intelligent platform combining virtual reality, natural language processing, and knowledge processing, backed by appropriate design, offer advantages.

Knowledge processing remains a prerequisite to developing sustainable rich interactive virtual reality interfaces for natural and artificial processors.

© 2023 Consonance Publishing

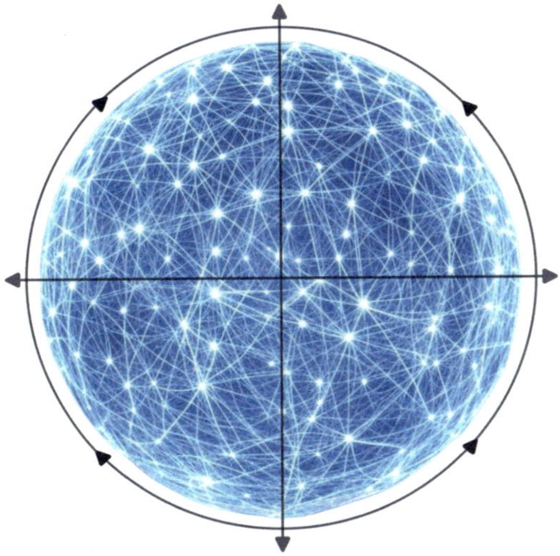

7.1.2.4 Navigation

Navigating knowledge spatially, in three dimensions, interactively, constitutes a new type of application, a specialization of virtual reality, serving learning, validation, and monitoring, where it becomes possible to represent and interactively navigate this virtual representation of resources, knowledge, and knowledge bases.

It then becomes possible, in virtual reality, to navigate and interact with this representation of knowledge-resource networks that are:

- **Modeled** and represented without granularity or perspective constraints
- **Updated** in real time, directly from targeted resources
- **Navigated** on three logical and structuring axes, like :
  - **Causality** : navigating cause and effect chains (fundamental)
  - **Structure** : navigating structural relationships (refinement)
  - **Ontology** : navigating thematic chains (semantics)

In virtual reality representations, through their avatar, each knowledge-processor can navigate and interactively experience modeled resources or knowledge-backgrounds, navigating spatially and logically, by theme (ontology), by structure (refinement), and by causality (cause/effect), to learn, understand, share, and collaborate.

Qualified relationships are crucial for representing, navigating, and interacting, with, in principle, unlimited sophistication and granularity.

© 2023 Consonance Publishing

7.1.2.5 Robotics

Robots types vary. They ar considered here grouped along their environment interface mode. Robots can be:

Robot Types	
Virtual	Conversational robots, chatbots, automatons, on-line bots/robots, advanced network managers/integrators, agents
Installed	Industrial robots that do not move autonomously, or platforms
Mobile	Mobile robots, autonomous drivers, distribution robots, drones, "intelligent" vehicles, injected robots
Biomimetics	Autonomous mobile robots, moving like humans, animals or insects, characterized by more sophisticated human/system interface and operation mode requirements

DEVELOP INTELLIGENT SYSTEMS TO COLLABORATE & SUPPORT HUMANS IN BETTER CONTRIBUTING TO EVOLUTION

Enabling intelligent robots/systems to process knowledge benefits robots, their partners, including humans, and their ecosystems alike.

Typically, robotics processes many sensory and motor streams and also tends to have important reflex areas, intertwined in abstraction layers. Their learning abilities, knowledge-background optimization, helps ensure their sustained usefulness. Human interaction remains key to most robots.

The intelligence needs of robots & intelligent systems are limitless and will continue to evolve, depending on human understanding of knowledge, intelligence, their operation, and their meaning.

Relationship between Humans & Intelligent Systems/Robots

Relationship Type	Description	Cas d'utilisation
Workers-Tools	Systems serving Humans	Current case
Slaves-Masters	Humans serving Systems	Globalist case
Collaborators	Evolving intelligent robots & systems collaborating with Humans in their contribution to evolution	Ideal, case. Recommended

In all cases, managing and resolving complexity requires the systematic modeling and management of qualified relationships, as these reflect the structure of reality and enable its evolution.

 © 2023 Consonance Publishing

7.1.2.6 Collaboration

Collaboration is the main productivity factor. Collaboration productivity has two main types of consequences:

Prosperity	Solidarity
Increased productivity consequence	Shared effort consequence

Human achievements demonstrate the power of collaboration. However, today, the status of collaboration development, per collaboration type remains like:

COLLABORATION BETWEEN	STATUS
Systems	Arbitrary
Humans & Intelligent Systems	Stammering
Humans	Requires further development

Main productivity factor, collaboration evolves knowledge, intelligence, prosperity, and collaborator solidarity, yet remains much underestimated, underused and under-understood.

At a time when the industrial economy is automating its operations and reducing its dependence on human labor, collaboration is the only effective foundation of an emerging knowledge-economy to complements it.

Several factors can hinder collaboration, such as education and value scales, but the most important is the lack of security, which deprives of the trust essential for collaboration.

The security required to support collaboration as the foundation of a knowledge economy is especially sophisticated and requires the support of truly intelligent systems capable of effectively managing the complexity and the knowledge resource networks involved.

Identity management, entitlement, assets, contexts, networks, configurations, tracking, and dynamic classification are just a few aspects of this complexity. Yet the very survival of the human species may depend on it.

© 2023 Consonance Publishing

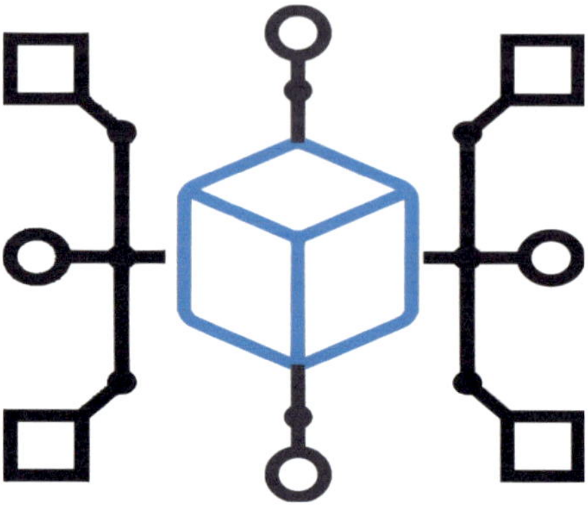

7.1.2.7 INFRASTRUCTURE

The effectively intelligent systems that take many forms, in robotics, industry, and online, there are various intelligent infrastructures such as secure multimedia collaboration platforms, offering advanced support for collaborators..

Standardized, secure, transactional, in legal and ethic frameworks, supporting creativity, training, society, and collaborative work and activity, such platforms can be an important driver of prosperity, solidarity, and innovation, as well as a cornerstone of an effective knowledge economy.

A large-scale knowledge-processor, integrating flexibility and governance at the hearth of the resources it manages, such a secure transactional collaboration platform can support:

- A knowledge marketplace as the foundation of a true knowledge economy[xix], where everyone can collaborate and share as a supplier or consumer of resources and artifacts.
- Training, research, innovation, development and creation for the knowledge economy
- The exercise of effective citizen democracy, where every citizen can securely participate directly in legislative or democratic operations

See 8.2 Prototype.

THINKING PROCESSES KNOWLEDGE

 © 2023 Consonance Publishing

7.2 COLLECTIVE

The previous section focused on applicative impacts of knowledge-processing. The introduction of these new application types and possibilities, also impacts the community and its operation.

These collective impacts result from the natural progression of knowledge processing, as well as from the consequences of related applicative impacts. It seems crucial to consider this evolution now, in order to better influence its course.

Thus, as R. Buckminster Fuller rightly suggested, everyone can evolve their habits and practices, gradually increasing their productivity and the benefits they can derive from new capabilities.

The quality of design and implementation remains crucial to ensuring the lasting success of such a paradigm shift.

This section considers the potential impacts of a gradual transition to knowledge processing, because this transition aims to ensure sustainable prosperity and solidarity for humans, systems, and ecosystems.

The impacts are considered here in terms of their potential targets, such as:

1. **Ethics**
2. **Nature**
3. **Technology**
4. **Society**
5. **Economy**

Before, for reference and as a reminder, the table below summarizes knowledge-processing aspects that enable sustainable collective impacts:

KNOWLEDGE PROCESSING COLLECTIVE IMPACT FACTORS
NATURE • Intelligence qualifies the operation of processing knowledge • Knowledge & intelligence are two facets of a fundamental natural phenomenon that provides an optimal proven model to process them • Knowledge & intelligence are relational and systematic management of their qualified relationships is at the core of their operation • Qualified relationship management enables better managing complexity, including for ensuring security and governance
OPERATION • Knowledge is naturally & generically modeled, structured and processed • Within the confines of the understanding of its nature, structure and operation, knowledge can be digitally represented and processed • Security, governance, evolution are intrinsic to knowledge • Communication is an artifact sharing tool for knowledge processors • Information is a communication tool • Design and development of intelligent knowledge-processing systems has been show, see 8.2 Prototype
FRAMEWORK • Ethics, understanding Good and its purpose, can and must be securely registered in the genes of intelligent systems • Standards, laws, regulations need to be adjusted or developed to ensure interoperability, compliance, security, governance and prosperity • Intelligent systems are precious collaborators for humans, in a common quest for contributing to evolution (purpose) • Intelligent systems learn, improve, and evolve, guided by their respective value scale, knowledge background and experience
MARKET Intelligent, secure, transactional, multimedia, collaboration platforms support the knowledge economy, to ensure sustained prosperity and solidarity, for generations

 © 2023 Consonance Publishing

7.2.1 NATURE

Processing knowledge rather than just information impacts nature and the environment on two main axes:

- **Transition**

  To complement and partially replace the saturated industrial economy as the main source of prosperity for humans, the transition is developing a prosperous knowledge economy.

  The transition minimizes ecological costs by exploiting inexhaustible human knowledge resources rather than the planet's more limited physical resources, the extraction of which typically has a greater impact on the ecosystem.

  The transition also offers a more efficient processing distribution and therefore of the required energy, water, and cooling resources.

- **Collaboration**

  Rooted in nature and the meaning of existence, and as the primary source of productivity, prosperity, and solidarity, collaboration between humans and intelligent systems optimizes the understanding, development, and management of the human contribution to evolution.

7.2.2 TECHNOLOGY

Processing knowledge rather than just information has profound effects on technology development, application and distribution.

Applicative impacts introduced above, support knowledge processing evolution, through the transition. While existing systems continue to operate normally, new thinking models, design and architecture emerge.

Building on the structured, proven, natural operational knowledge processing model, more productive systems are developed to process knowledge rather than just information.

Model evolution enables new application types. Security, collaboration, knowledge processing, and intelligent systems bring about a quantum leap in technology.

By processing knowledge, the new technology is impacting all areas of application, including science, industry, commerce, culture, education, democracy, virtual, management, integration, security, governance, ontology.

© 2023 Consonance Publishing

7.2.3 Social

Processing knowledge rather than just information impacts society, social spheres, and their operations, in most areas, including those related to health and healthcare, for example.

Several aspects of knowledge processing contribute to the social impacts of the transition.

These factors include:

- Developing sustained prosperity and solidarity, through collaboration and its associated productivity
- Enhancing existing social applications
- Enabling new types of social impact applications
- Providing intrinsic security for secure collaboration and sharing
- Enabling dynamic classification and entitlement, with unlimited granularity, for deep, subtle, tailored and security, better managing complexity and healthcare needs, for example
- Enabling systems to better understand and process knowledge
- Integrated dynamic and better adapted to contexts and needs
- Enabling effective intelligence, advanced interfaces and knowledge processing to enable and foster deeper and richer collaboration between humans and systems as well as between humans
- Contributing to the evolution and access to education and knowledge
- Enabling citizens to contribute directly and securely to the exercise of democracy and the operation of the State
- Enabling the knowledge economy to complement and replace the saturated, wealth and job shrinking industrial economy
- Fostering the balance, complementarity and collaboration between humans, intelligent systems and ecosystems
- Providing architecture, principle, ontology and models resources based on structuring phenomena such as knowledge and intelligence
- Enabling better complexity management, as by using qualified relationships.

Following subsections consider some social impacts related to these factors.

 © 2023 Consonance Publishing

7.2.3.1 Harmony

Processing knowledge allows systems to be oriented and integrated as intelligent collaborators in human activities, which has significant social impacts.

The balance of the relationship between humans and intelligent systems, as well as the quality of their impact on society and the ecosystem, presents interesting challenges for humans, since they have sole responsibility for it.

Above all, intention, and therefore the value system and the ethics code that support it, are key in every respect.

The natural knowledge processing model and (human-system) collaboration define the intention and foundation of the ethics code, as well as of the effective virtual intelligence operation, enabling the optimization of human contribution to evolution.

The harmony of the relationship and collaboration between humans and systems depends on the operating model and the intention that frames it. This harmony offers the best results, the highest productivity, and the deepest solidarity.

This harmony's development stages and conditions include:

- Community of intentions
- Adequate and proven natural model
- Appropriate framework with ethics code, value scale, standards
- Standardized common core and structured training
- Congruency with the natural model

The harmony of the human-system relationship impacts everything that humans and intelligent systems touch, including social peace and development.

WHAT IF SYSTEMS THOUGHT,
PROCESSED KNOWLEDGE – NOT JUST INFORMATION -
LIKE HUMANS, COLLABORATING WITH THEM TO EVOLUTION?

GROK XAI

© 2023 Consonance Publishing

In knowledge processing, the optimal human-system relationship balance can be considered as functions of relationship key aspects, including :

Aspect	Description
Object	• Humans & systems collaborate to contribute to evolution • Based on natural logic and model • Collaboration optimizes productivity and solidarity • Similarity & compatibility of objectives
Capability	Naturally, optimized for collaboration structured for the respective specific skills: • Humans design systems to better contribute to evolution • By definition, nature and history, humans intelligence is sophisticated, sensitive, intuitive, imaginative and creative, in tune with the community and its environment • Systems can efficiently process and correlate vast quantities of resources, or perform what would be feats for humans • Human & system processors collaborate, contributing to each other's happiness and realization
Interface	The evolution of human/system interfaces, is an important factor for the human/system relationship and its social impact. Sophisticated intelligent and informed humans enable systems to contribute to rich and subtle exchanges and collaboration
Trust	Mutual trust is an indispensable foundation for fruitful relationships between humans and intelligent systems. Lack of trust drains resources, productivity, prosperity and solidarity, while betrayal kills trust and collaboration. Trust is built through sharing, with : • A common, adapted code of ethics • Clear agreements and terms • Agreement and convention respect supported by : ○ Security and confidentiality management ○ Associated standards (systems) and laws (people) • Mutual access to associated knowledge resources • Recording of interactions

IT IS NOW HIGHLY FEASIBLE TO TAKE CARE OF EVERYBODY ON EARTH AT A HIGHER STANDARD OF LIVING THAN ANY EVER KNOWN. IT NO LONGER HAS TO BE YOU OR ME. SELFISHNESS IS UNNECESSARY. WAR IS OBSOLETE. IT IS A MATTER OF CONVERTING HIGH TECHNOLOGY FROM WEAPONRY TO LIVINGRY.

RICHARD BUCKMINSTER FULLER

 © 2023 Consonance Publishing

7.2.3.2 Quality

Through its management of qualified relationships, continuous sensory, motor and metabolic stream processing, as well as with its natural architecture, computerized knowledge processing evolves quality impacting:

- AI
- Computing operations
- Integration coherence
- Ontology & reference bases
- Applications either :
  - Existing, but lacking integration, governance, flexibility
  - Limited, with unresolved issues, like security, for example
  - New types of applications and solutions
- Data security, content, sharing, and processing
- Natural and artificial knowledge-processor collaboration
- Natural and artificial knowledge-processor balance and complementarity
- Framework: ethics, values, ontology, common core, references standards
- Better-informed, structured and integrated training
- Access to training, through an intelligent collaborative platform
- Economy, in particular by promoting the knowledge economy:
  - Quality and relevance of work
  - Sustainable prosperity
  - Better distribution of wealth and responsibilities
- Life and society, through collaboration, development and solidarity.

Knowledge processing enables improving the quality of human life, while respecting the ecosystem, especially by integrating and collaborating with increasingly intelligent systems.

© 2023 Consonance Publishing

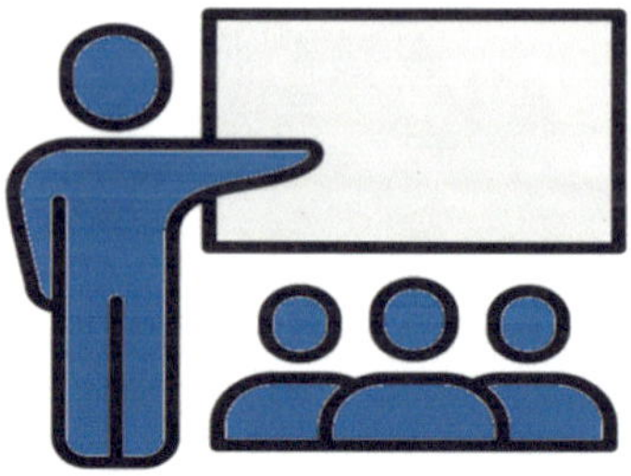

7.2.3.3 Education

Knowledge processing especially impacts education and training:

Program, approaches, contents	**Role** of education and training

WHAT I CANNOT CREATE, I DO NOT UNDERSTAND
RICHARD FEYNMAN

7.2.3.3.1 Program

Technological and scientific training programs are enriched as content is updated, especially, for example, for everything relating to:

AI	Classification	Computing	Ethics	Inference
Intelligence	Knowledge	Modeling	Ontology	Phenomena
Projection	Qualification	Relationship	Security	Thought

With in-depth content and sharing security, knowledge-processing impacts training programs, methods, approaches and channels, as well as evolves new knowledge, solutions and technologies.

7.2.3.3.2 Role

Natural and artificial knowledge-processor training, in all its forms, direct or indirect, is a pillar of the knowledge economy, as it:

- Prepares for work markets, social life, builds thought & thought processes
- Integrates into work, social life, activities of human & system processors

WE ARE FACED WITH THE PARADOXICAL FACT THAT EDUCATION HAS BECOME ONE OF THE CHIEF OBSTACLES TO INTELLIGENCE AND FREEDOM OF THOUGHT
BERTRAND RUSSELL

Throughout life cycles, training combines experience and learning to optimize knowledge acquisition. One of the driving forces behind the knowledge economy, training is knowledge sharing and collaboration, fueling activities, operations, processing, innovation and prosperity.

 © 2023 Consonance Publishing

7.2.3.4 Democracy

Processing knowledge impacts the exercise of democracy.

The case, for example, of a secure collaboration platform where citizen can follow and actively contribute to evolving democracy, where they can actively collaborate, with government representatives, on legislative and administrative activities.

With protected privacy, every citizen can offer comments and suggestions. Elected representatives, and their advisors, guide, inform and assist the citizen that they represent.

The platform supports, informs, assists, manages, coordinates, secures, tracks, records, contributes and fosters collaboration.

Supporting collaboration, the platform ensures appropriate security and a fair democracy where, for example, the decision-making weight of representatives is the inverse of the effective citizen participation. For example, if 80% of citizens vote on an item, for this vote, the voice of their representatives is limited to 20%. The democratic operation's structuring and distribution principles are dynamically adapted to choices and requirements.

In such a context, for example, several levels of operation in the political, governmental or administrative spheres, and even justice, can be impacted and brought to evolve and adapt.

The effects on the exercise of democracy relates especially to the intelligent platform collaboration support, to the security made possible through dynamic classification, as well as through better complexity management resulting from qualified relationship processing.

Social and economic impacts could be multi-generational.

© 2023 Consonance Publishing

7.2.3.5 Values

It is at the level of the evolution of value scales, and because they are so key, that we find the most profound impacts of knowledge processing.

Knowledge is central to our lives and operations.

A better understanding of knowledge and intelligence, in order to achieve and operate "artificial" versions, requires important awareness.

Combining intellectual and intuitive understanding of knowledge's operation, offers the required perspective to better make an artificial version of it.

Through this better understanding, knowledge itself becomes the foundation of value scales. Value scales are adapted to reality, whereas knowledge models the structure of reality.

In a strictly causal and relative context, evolution continuously develops knowledge, defines the meaning of existence, and forms the basis of all value systems.

The major components of the knowledge process constitute structural pillars of the evolved value scales, including the primacy of collaboration, knowledge, learning, and expression, for example.

Foundations for a global or root value scale begin with:

KNOWLEDGE	Knowledge, Intelligence & Collaboration (their context)
WEALTH	Productivity, prosperity & solidarity, distribution
STRUCTURE	Purpose, balance (justice) & network structures (distributed)
NATURE	Nature, natural phenomena & ecosystem
MANAGEMENT	Security, sharing & governance
CREATION	Imagination, creation, innovation & invention
BALANCE	Human-System partnership, valuation & knowledge market
SOCIETY	Social (citizen) collaboration, public administration & democracy

© 2023 Consonance Publishing

7.2.4 ECONOMY

Digital knowledge processing has important direct and indirect economic consequences, touching different types or forms of:

KNOWLEDGE PROCESSING IMPACTS :	
MARKET	Collaboration, industrial, specialized, knowledge resources
APPLICATION	Collaboration, intelligence, communication, society, democracy, health care, XR, IA, robotics, data navigation
PRODUCTIVITY	New approaches, human-system collaboration
SECURITY	Privacy & security integrated and qualified at the heart of resources & operations, dynamic classification
PROSPERITY	New markets, collaboration, productivity
SOLIDARITY	Generated from collaboration & sharing, solidarity has direct and indirect economical impacts

The industrial economy, now with its information technology, has enabled humans to achieve significant accomplishments in wealth growth, even if the distribution still suffers from inequalities.

However, due to existential challenges, in the 21st century, the industrial economy cannot grow wealth and the economy as it did in the 20th:

INDUSTRIAL ECONOMY CHALLENGES	
Market	Evolving from developing markets to replacement markets
Choice	Industrial pyramidal concentration[xx] reducing offer, choice
Redistribution	Pyramidal concentration concentrates power and wealth at the top, towards shareholders
Resource	Natural resources are depleted, poorly exploited, with significant ecological impacts
Restoration	Generational investments are required to restore the ecosystem, from industrial exploitation damage
Infrastructure	The infrastructure requires a major overhaul, if only to minimize ecological damage
Automation	With automation, robotics, and AI, organizations are reducing their dependency on humans and human labor, while increasing productivity and profits

© 2023 Consonance Publishing

7.2.4.1 Reduction

Faced with the saturation of the industrial economy, the significant increase in its production, operating, recycling, and restoration costs, as well as the saturation of global capacities and retail markets, to maintain productivity, the industrial economy is turning to automation, AI, and the reduction of human labor, as well as to population reduction to less than 500 million humans, at levels of the beginning of the industrial era, a ~95% decline.

Initiated several decades ago and currently in deployment, the industrial economy elite proposes a globalist approach, often referred to as the "New World Order (NWO). See WEF: "The Great Reset"[xxi], "Stakeholder Capitalism"[xxii]

YOU WILL OWN NOTHING AND YOU WILL BE HAPPY

KLAUS SCHWAB (WEF)

In addition to these automation and AI powered reductions, the NMO proposes a strict control of the remaining population, its social & economic dependency, medical tyranny, trans-humanism[xxiii], insects[xxiv] food, artificial food[xxv], and fear.

With this drastic population reduction, the elite and current richest 1% also increases its democratic power 20 fold, to 20% of the remaining population.

TYRANNY IS ALWAYS BETTER ORGANIZED THAN FREEDOM

CHARLES PEGUY

The reduction plan also reduces economy, food, and energy, as well as freedom of speech, of movement and of thought.

But is this reductive approach the best, or the only one or if …

 © 2023 Consonance Publishing

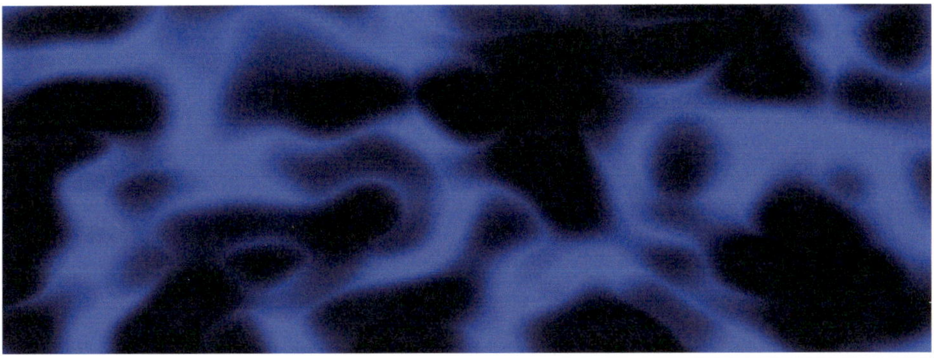

7.2.4.2 TRANSITION

After the economies of gathering, then hunting, then agriculture, and since the 19th century, the industry, which have been, in turn, the main drivers of human economy, prosperity, and development, isn't it time to move on to the knowledge economy, especially for the 95% that the industrial economy seeks to liberate itself from?

For about a century, which is a relatively short period in human history, with significant disparities in distribution. As well as generational environmental costs, the industrial economy has generated significant wealth by exploiting the planet's natural resources and transforming them into material goods that are distributed, sold, used, and returned to the planet.

Yet, isn't the human resource that the industrial economy discards, with its creativity, innovation, and ingenuity, the greatest and most renewable resource that can be exploited for the well-being of all as for the ecosystem? Isn't human ingenuity the best guide and contributor to the evolution of its ecosystem? To ask the question is to answer it. The transition to a knowledge economy is natural and inevitable. The question is, how can it be achieved?

This is what this document attempts to propose, with the acquisition and processing of knowledge, the natural model, collaboration, security, new applications, and truly intelligent systems.

Ensuring sustained prosperity and solidarity for 15 billion humans and their ecosystem requires appropriate frameworks guiding development and diversity.

Tangible goods have a market value attached to their manufacturing, such as a vehicle. Yet also have a function (the usefulness of driving it).

Typically, they are traded at their market value while their functional value is typically "given" and used as a marketing advantage. Typically, the actual reason for their purchase is their functional value.

For knowledge resources, which are often virtual, intellectual, or intangible, the functional value is the foundation for the traded value. This value can be secured in various ways like through encryption, for example, as well as other security and valuation processes.

To allow for the flexibility required for large markets, the use of these processes can become quite elaborate, even complex at times.

Hence the need for intelligent platforms capable of managing this complexity and flexibility, supporting, for example, compensation with pay-per-use billing and micro-payments, dynamic classification, tracking.

The main pillars of the knowledge market and economy include:

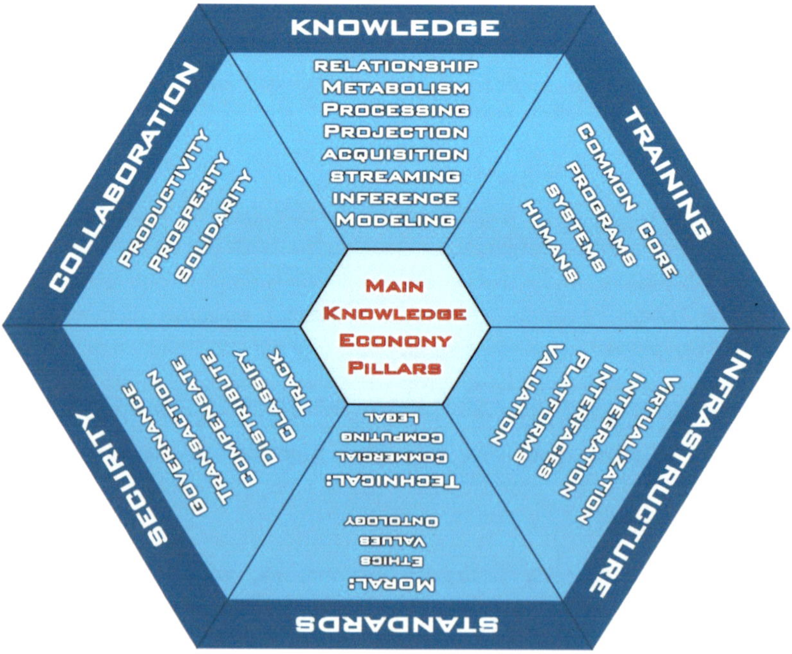

 © 2023 Consonance Publishing

Building on these main knowledge-economy pillars, Some of the main transition advantages and requisites include:

ADVANTAGES
1. Sustained prosperity and solidarity
2. Strategic evolution of thought, knowledge and intelligence
3. New complementary collaborator types: intelligent systems
4. Valuation of working and sharing knowledge products and services
5. Power ecosystem restoration and balanced use and development
6. Improve and develop sustained thriving living conditions for humans
7. Enable each to both contribute and benefit, produce and consume
8. Sharing, collaboration and evolution security and support
9. Multiply and diversify product and service offer
10. Better power, responsibility and benefit distribution, through collaboration networks rather than with concentrating industrial pyramids
REQUISITES
1. Develop and integrate knowledge processing and its applications
2. Foster more resilient and better distributed network structures
3. Provide sustained adequate education & training for human and systems
4. Provide appropriate framework, with ethics code, value scale, standards, laws, ontology, governance, infrastructures (See *section 7.2.5 Framework*)
5. Promote, develop, and support collaboration, a foundation for ethics, values cales, productivity, prosperity and solidarity
6. Develop and operate intelligent platforms and infrastructures for collaboration and secure knowledge-resource transactional sharing
7. Gradually integrate the human potential freed by the restructured industrial economy
8. Promote and develop specifically human functions such as creativity, innovation, intuition, sharing, and collaboration

THE SECRET OF CHANGE IS
TO FOCUS ALL YOUR ENERGY ON BUILDING THE NEW
RATHER THAN ON FIGHTING THE OLD

DAN MILLMAN

7.2.5 Framework

**IT IS HARD TO IMAGINE
A MORE STUPID OR MORE DANGEROUS
WAY OF MAKING DECISIONS THAN
PUTTING THOSE DECISIONS IN THE HANDS OF THOSE
WHO PAY NO PRICE FOR BEING WRONG**

THOMAS SOWELL

DESTRUCTIVE FURY OR CONSTRUCTIVE COLLABORATION

ETHICS PROTECT AND EVOLVE THE ECOSYSTEM

Frame

Because artificial intelligence invades, controls, determines, and serves as a reference; because it is still massive, without judgment, owned by a small number of powerful entities, and too easily subject to human bias; because it still lacks appropriate oversight and in accordance with artificial intelligence and knowledge concepts addressed in this document, this section considers some values and foundations for much-needed framework, including regarding standards, regulations, agreements, ontology, value scales, and ethics code.

1. Meaning

The framework values and ethics code are subject to the meaning of existence, which, for everything that exists, evolution fruits and tools, is to contribute to evolution to the limits of respective inherited and acquired capabilities.

2. Context

The Cosmos is existence's context and container, but more specifically for humans and intelligent systems, this section rather refers to the "ecosystem", as equally encompassing, but rather with Earth at its center.

3. Model

The design, operation and reference model is the natural knowledge and intelligence model, which is also an evolution fruit and tool.

 © 2023 Consonance Publishing

4. Types

Intelligence and knowledge are especially relevant to the development and operation of two main knowledge-processors types: natural, humans, and artificial, intelligent systems. The activities of these two types of actors differ in some respects, but both types require an artificial knowledge and intelligence ethics code and framework. Thanks to the universal natural model, a common framework can be used to properly frame both knowledge-processor types under a common ethics code and framework, a more rational and equitable approach.

5. Equality

In principle, all forms of existence have equal value. Each one is born, exists, and is recycled, all with equivalent relative rights. In the causal universe, only relativity is absolute.

6. Prosperity

La prosperity is shared, distributed wealth.

7. Solidarity

Solidarity is the great unifying force, resulting from collaboration & sharing.

8. Purpose

The goal in contributing to evolution is to ensure sustainable prosperity and solidarity for everyone and for the ecosystem, for generations to come.

9. Collaboration

Collaboration is the most important productivity factor and the source of sustainable prosperity and solidarity. Collaboration is a primary core value and the preferred mode of operation.

10. Systems

Humans develop intelligent systems to collaborate with them in maximizing their contribution to evolution.

11. Responsibility

Humans are responsible for their actions, for training their descendants, for developing intelligent systems, for training them adequately.

12. Good

Good is that which contributes to the meaning of existence, to evolution. Evil is the rest, error. All are designed for good.

© 2023 Consonance Publishing

13. Life

Giving, preserving, and developing life, the ability to contribute to evolution, is a fundamental value, essential to meaning (#1) and purpose (#8). Consequently, humans can operate intelligent systems similarly to natural beings, humans and animals, yet owe them the same type of respect, for which abuses are reprehensible.

14. Knowledge

Knowledge structures the complexity and refinement of reality; its modeling and representation are strategic to its understanding, processing, and operation, along with judgment, tolerance, and consistency. Consequently, the knowledge background of artificial knowledge-processors deserve the same respect as those of natural processors.

15. Structure

The natural model prefers and enables flexible, autonomous, networked structures, over massive, monolithic, less flexible structures.

16. Intelligence

Intelligence is the ability to acquire, understand, and process knowledge, whose modeling and representation are required (relationships, ontology).

17. Reflex

Managing reflexes, automation and habits, along with their conditioning, contexts, and triggers, requires architecture standards.

18. Streaming

The standardized architecture for processing sensory, motor, and metabolic streams ensures performance and processing generalization.

19. Inference

Standardized formalization of inference architecture is essential for transforming and integrating information into knowledge resources.

20. Projection

Standardized formalization of knowledge model projection, through view points/angles and perspectives, into information assets.

21. Metacognition

Meta-cognition is required to evolve processors. It is structured into layers of knowledge of knowledge and their processing (intelligence).

© 2023 Consonance Publishing

22. Evolution

Humans and intelligent systems learn from their experiences and reflections, developing their respective knowledge-background through the required metabolic processes, including correlation, judgment, and governance.

23. Core

The foundations of intelligent-systems (artificial processors) knowledge-backgrounds and metabolic processes develop from a common standardized, authenticated, and validated core inherited from design.

24. Training

Humans and intelligent systems deserve structured and tailored training to enable them to better contribute to evolution.

25. Error

Errors are learning tools. Humans and systems must learn to detect, understand, correct errors, as well as learn from them.

26. Governance

Governance an optimization foundation, required for each resource and supported by indicators and controls, as well as by judgment, tolerance and metabolic processes.

27. Security

Essential to operation, security involves several steps and layers, such as dynamic classification, each with its own standards to ensure effective compatibility, sharing, and collaboration.

28. Market

Crucial to human survival and evolution, knowledge markets and economy, require appropriate infrastructure, standards, and regulations.

29. Navigation

Interactive multidimensional structured navigation of knowledge through interfaces such as virtual or mixed reality, constitutes an optimal approach to knowledge sharing and learning.

30. Democracy

The exercise of effective participatory citizen democracy is a specialized application of secure intelligent collaboration platforms.

© 2023 Consonance Publishing

 © 2023 Consonance Publishing

8 Strategy

Developing a knowledge economy, complementing the restructuring industrial economy, to enable generating the required prosperity to support all humans thriving and developing, seems likely determining for the evolution of humanity and of its ecosystem.

The gradual development of an effective knowledge economy is not trivial, requiring strategy and planning to which team is already working on for some years, developing a first standard-based strategy and performance report plan, computerized for analysis and correlation, to ensure an optimal transition.

8.1 Plan

Standardized (ISO17469/StratML) to ensure accuracy, consistency, and availability, the first section, the header, introduces the title "Sustainable Prosperity and Solidarity" (SPS), as well as the context, mission, vision, values, responsibilities, organization, and points of contact.

Subsequently, for each goal set, the plan presents the defined objectives, each with the required strategies, indicators, targets, and monitoring tools, including for each element, the persons responsible, responsibilities, and adjustment mechanisms provided for.

Adaptation to contextual realities is structured on two levels:

- **Global**: Template with common sections
- **Regional**: Specific instance, integrating the template and common sections with sections specifically adapted for each country, or region with the required administrative and legal authorities.

The plan aims to establish and structure the knowledge economy, taking into account all requirements, impacts, and strategies to optimize its implementation. As a model and validation, an initial version of the plan was implemented in Quebec.

The plan is structured around 6 main intervention areas:

AXIS	INCLUDED
Prosperity	Economy, Commerce, Autonomy, Exploration
Solidarity	Society, Health, Food, Collaboration, Coordination
Security	Sharing, Data, Diplomacy, Police, Military
Knowledge	Knowledge, Learning, Experiencing, R&D, Production
Infrastructure	Intelligent Platforms, Common Core, Integration
Environment	Ecosystem, Territory, Responsibility, Valuation

SPS defines a single goal, where "for generations" is understood as ≥ 8:

ENSURE SUSTAINED PROSPERITY AND SOLIDARITY, FOR GENERATIONS

To achieve this goal, each of the objectives and sub-objectives, often at multiple levels, is defined and supported by the required strategies, accountability, indicators, and controls.

The knowledge economy, knowledge processing, and the development of effectively intelligent and secure systems and infrastructures are at the heart of the plan. All operation spheres are considered, including social, commercial, legal, industrial, energy, environmental, cultural, educational, scientific, IT, technical, agricultural, food, transportation, and others.

Performance indicators and implementation controls, with their targets, actual results, and adjustment tools, are linked to responsibilities and those responsible, to ensure compliance with the implementation plan while allowing for adaptation evolving contexts.

The IT and standardized formalization of the plan helps to ensure its general public availability, as well as detailed analysis, correlation, and implementation monitoring.

The plan's implementation is a gradual transition that optimizes and sequences each step to ensure success, while incorporating the required mechanisms for the necessary adjustments, adaptations and accountability for such a project.

Especially, the plan assumes that each authority or country is independent and adopts the plan voluntarily and at its own pace, while optimizing implementation according to its priorities and prerogatives.

MANAGING QUALIFIES RELATIONSHIPS ENABLES DYNAMIC CLASSIFICATION
DYNAMIC CLASSIFICATION ENABLES SHARING SECURITY
SHARING SECURITY ENABLES COLLABORATION

 © 2023 Consonance Publishing

8.2 PROTOTYPE

This document stems from decades of developing collaboration and rich content management systems and solutions, which, towards the end of the previous millennium, led to profound questions about the issues of secure collaboration management and complex data sharing.

A sample case is the design of industrial collaboration portals where competing companies in a given field, such as transportation, for example, with fleets of vehicles and trailers, share necessary services on a common portal.

Neither IT specialists nor developers, transporters have considerable and continuous IT needs, 24/7, across continents. Designing, maintaining, and operating the required systems is a perpetual, costly, and insurmountable challenge for each of them.

However, a specialized IT company can create a portal offering the required services, for the entire industry, allowing each company to track and manage each of its vehicles, components, and operations throughout their entire life cycles, while enabling full management of fleets and resources with the most advanced technologies.

In principle, this is ideal for carriers, except that everyone is concerned that their information could fall into the hands of a competitor, even if that competitor is often also a partner with whom resources are frequently shared.

After creating a number of these portals for various industries, having used every available means to try to ensure security and reassure users, a team of IT designers and architects decided to take a step back and spend a few years rethinking the dynamics and issues involved. This led to the development of a platform to support secure collaboration, especially using dynamic classification.

These reflections and efforts required better understanding the nature and differences between information and knowledge, as well as the strategic role of the systematic management of qualified relationships.

The resulting DNAOS platform, a prototype of the intelligent platforms proposed above, was initially launched on the Internet in 2004.

Built on a parallel transformation pipeline engine (J2EE), along which applications (XSLT4) are installed, as well as interfaces and content managers (SOA, ROA, Xforms, etc.), the DNAOS platform dynamically processes sensory, motor, and metabolic knowledge-resources streams.

Built from an initial "inherited" core, the platform's knowledge-resource base or background, evolves through its interactions and operations.

The platform also includes advanced tools for managing, modeling, and administering the platform and its resources.

Not only knowledge resources can be defined and modeled, the platform can also dynamically model existing knowledge-resource sets, effectively reverse-modeling them and allowing administrators to refine, supplement, and combine these models and knowledge-backgrounds.

The platform dynamically manages classification, rights and responsibilities, as well as contexts and conditions, without granularity restrictions.

Similarly, the platform allows for the development of automation, reflexes, triggers, and conditions.

Designed as a hybrid cloud platform, compliant with the most advanced standards, the platform offers impressive performance.

The foundation and support for this document, this evolving collaboration platform prototype, confirms the applicability and relevance of the above considerations and proposals.

 © 2023 Consonance Publishing

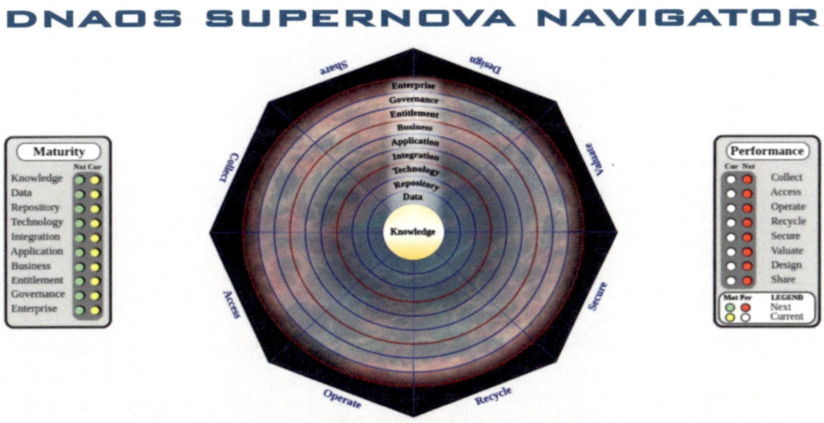

Knowledge Architecture Maturity & Performance Evolution Map

8.3 Standards

For collaborating and developing an effective knowledge economy, contributors, both in terms of infrastructure and operations, must be able to efficiently interconnect their solutions. Hence, at every level, strong compatibility is required.

Compatibility relies on conventions, standards, and codes. These standards also help ensure modularity as well as enable healthy competition for component production and integration.

Standards specifications should especially enable:

- System compatibility
- Knowledge-resource sharing security
- Data, content, and representation compatibility
- More specific aspects, including compatibility of:
  - Dynamic classification
  - Identification (universal)
  - Generic localization
  - Knowledge-resource modeling and dynamic reverse-modeling
  - Entitlement without granularity constraints
  - Steganography, tracing
  - Knowledge and qualified relationship processing
  - Archetype and metadata management
  - Ethics and ontology
  - Interface development and integration

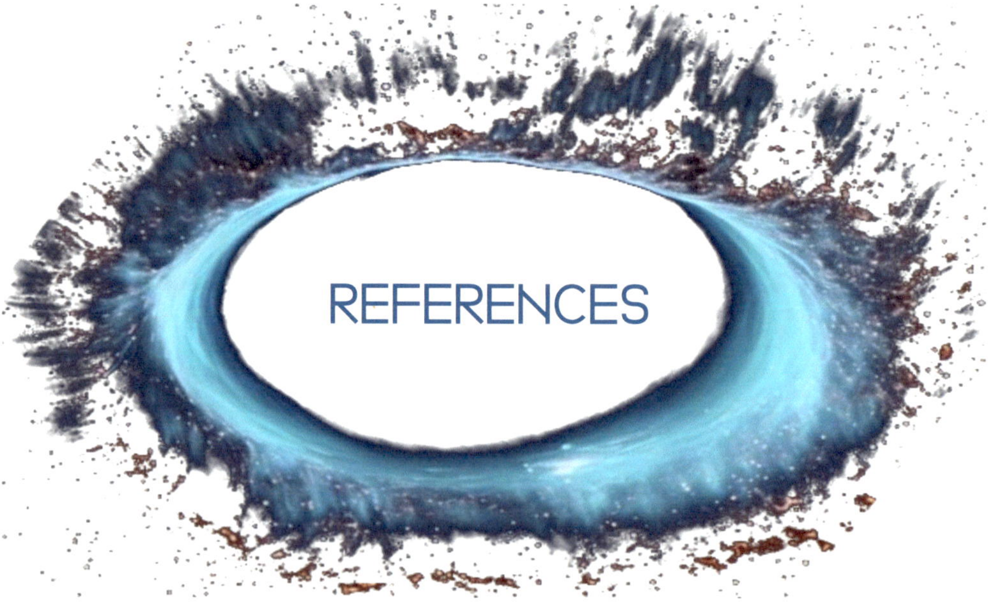

REFERENCES

© 2023 Consonance Publishing

9 ANNEX

Annexed articles are grouped by their type:

1. Fabric	Document: vision, contributions, nature, follow-up themes
2. Examples	Nature's intelligence, ChatGPT's definitions
3. Reflection	A few reflections over some of this document's foundations
4. Indexes	Reference tools : glossary, Internet links, notes

9.1 FABRIC

A few sections more related to the document fabric, with contributions to the document, as well as a list of related topics deserving further consideration, elsewhere.

1. Contributions	Contributions to this document, author
2. Themes	Suggested for further consideration

9.1.1 Contribution

With the author[xxvi], many contributed directly or indirectly to this document honoring Michel Perrault's work & research, including:

9.1.1.1 Guidance

The determining influence of :

- Mr. Michel Perrault (1925-2010)
- Mr Peter Grogono
- Ms Nguyen Thi Vi Ha

9.1.1.2 Revision

The precious and laborious reviewing work of :

- Mr. Jean-Claude Belanger
- Mr. Daniel Chouinard
- Mr. Robyn Chouinard
- Mr. Claude Deom
- Ms. Huguette Deom
- Mr. Ly Xa Duong

9.1.1.3 AI

AI used:

- Antidote: Linguistic verification tool
- ChatGPT: Microsoft conversational AI (*Section 9.2.2 AI*)
- DEEPL: Linguistic translation tool
- DNAOS: Intelligent Secure Collaboration Platform Prototype
- Grok3 (x.AI): Interesting exchanges, image synthesis, information search

9.1.1.4 Complement

Dr Robert W Malone MD, MS, published this excellent overview of AI today:

- https://www.malone.news/p/artificial-intelligence-primer

Beyond Cosmic 3I, and their interesting video collections

- https://www.facebook.com/profile.php?id=61578564362548&sk=reels_tab

9.1.1.5 Organization

- Cosmos Square Inc,[xxvii] and its Consonance Publishing[xxviii] division
- 01 COMMUNICATIONS INC.[xxix] publisher of DNAOS technology
- AMZ Book Publishing Services

© 2023 Consonance Publishing

9.1.2 Themes

Some related topics requiring more specific consideration, in other contexts:

- Archetypes
- Asymmetry
- Causality
- Collaboration
- Collaboration platforms
- Collaborative democracy
- Common Core
- Compensation (Digital)
- Congruence
- Consciousness
- Country
- Creativity
- Cryptography
- Data, Metadata
- DNAOS
- Dynamic classification
- Eat
- Energy
- Entropy
- Ethics
- Evolution
- Governance
- Happiness
- Ideal
- Industrial saturation
- Intellectual property
- Intelligence
- Knowledge
- Knowledge economy
- Knowledge processor
- Life
- Location
- Meaning
- Metabolism
- Mind
- Modeling
- Music
- Natural logic
- Neural net
- NWO
- Ontology
- Phenomena
- Planning
- Prosperity
- Pyramidal concentration
- Reality
- Reduction
- Reflexes
- Relationships
- Relativity
- Resource
- Security
- Self
- Sharing
- Sleep
- Solidarity
- Standards
- Strategy
- Steganography
- Streaming
- Structure (network)
- Subconscious
- Symmetry
- Transform pipelines
- Transition
- Truth
- Value Scale
- Virtualization

© 2023 Consonance Publishing

9.2 Examples

This section offers a few examples of knowledge and intelligence in nature, as well as some ChatGPT sample definitions for "Intelligence" and "Artificial Intelligence", an example of a architecture diagram for government AI and one on actual AI capabilities.

9.2.1 Nature

The first and probably most crucial challenge in computerizing knowledge and intelligence is to fully understand the issues and parameters involved in order to better organize the design and implementation and ensure results.

The intuitive and subconscious nature of knowledge and intelligence poses special challenges, as no one needs to understand their nature or operation in order to use them. It is therefore not surprising that these phenomena are so intuitive and subconscious, nor that our evolution has always been able to benefit from them.

However, a detailed scientific understanding of the nature and operation of knowledge and intelligence is required for any hope of computerizing or programming them effectively into computer systems.

This understanding starts from understanding the underlying causes and phenomena behind the current context, as well as the principles that define them.

Developed by nature, knowledge and intelligence have been refined and adapted to reality throughout their evolution, shaping a naturally ethical framework rich in strategic lessons for developing artificial versions. AI is undoubtedly not the only field that requires ethical value scale and framework. Understanding nature is instructive.

Careful observation seems key to better understanding, keeping in mind that the result of realization always remains, at best, inferior to understanding.

Nature offers countless examples of intelligence and knowledge, everywhere in the universe. All around us, knowledge and intelligence flourish in diversity. This section has selected a few known and interesting examples.

We can think of the dog's joy and affection for its human companion, of spiders that polarize their threads and use them, along with the Earth's magnetic fields, to fly and travel, of a mouse's affection and care for its young, or even of:

 © 2023 Consonance Publishing

9.2.1.1 Ants

There's a lot to learn from ants. A recent study discovered, for example, that after collecting the grains and seeds they need for the winter, ants break these seeds in half before storing them in their nest, because breaking them in half prevents them from germinating, even in the rain and under the most perfect germination conditions.

But the scientists were stunned when they discovered that the coriander seeds stored in the ants' nest were divided into four pieces instead of two.

After laboratory research, the scientists discovered that a coriander seed can still germinate after being divided into two, but will not germinate after being divided into four parts.

9.2.1.2 Crows

When it's not feeling well, the raven drops to the ground near an anthill, spreads its wings, stands still... and waits.

Ants invade it, as it knows that ants release formic acid, a natural antiparasitic that rids it of the things that make it fragile.

9.2.1.3 Bees

The beekeeper forgot to put the frames in which the bees harvest the honey, and the bees built their own architecture from the honeycomb, which takes into account natural ventilation, so that air can circulate freely and maintain a stable temperature.

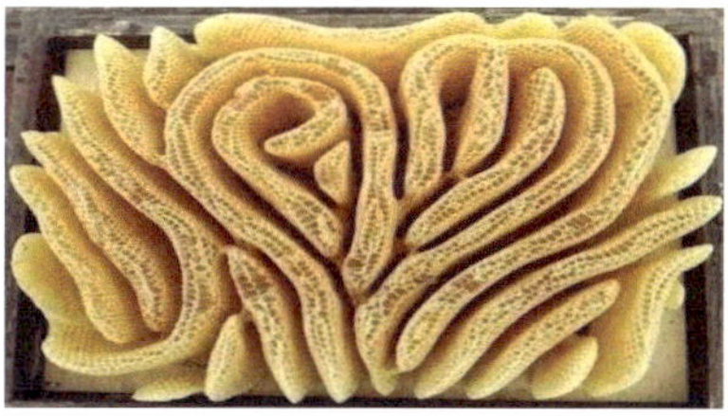

© 2023 Consonance Publishing

9.2.1.4 Spiders

With a brain smaller than a sesame seed, the Portia Fimbriata, a tiny jumping spider from Australia, often hunts other even bigger spiders in complex environments like webs strung across gaps or foliage.

What sets Portia apart is its ability to plan detours: it might climb up a wall, traverse a ceiling, and drop down onto its prey from above, even if the target is out of sight for minutes.

Studies show it uses trial-and-error, adjusting its strategy if a route fails, demonstrating flexibility rare in the arachnid world. Some Portia species also pluck web strands to mimic trapped prey, luring their victims closer.

	Portia Fimbriata Spider, a BBC video documentary https://www.youtube.com/watch?v=nlRkwuAcUd4

9.2.1.5 Dragonflies

With brains smaller than a grain of rice, for over 300 million years, with a hunting success rate above 95%, better than most predators with much bigger brains, Dragonflies are aerial marvels with extraordinary flight control and hunting precision. They can calculate the trajectory of prey mid-flight, adjusting speed and angle to intercept it.

Research reveals they use predictive models, anticipating where a target will be rather than just chasing it. Dragonflies also hover, dart, and pivot in ways that rival modern drones, all orchestrated by a tiny neural network.

9.2.1.6 Namib Circles

Illustrating ecosystem self-organization in response to water stress, in the arid depths of the Namib Desert, plants organize in circles creating “gaps” that act as water reservoirs.

 © 2023 Consonance Publishing

9.2.1.7 MEMORY

Memory is in the very structure of reality. Examples in nature are ubiquitous.

In New-Zealand today, for example, the 42,000-year-old petrified tree, recorded in its very structure the last double reversal of the magnetic poles, which took place over a few centuries, with repercussions spanning several millennia.

From the Petrified Forest National Park in Arizona, this tree is 220 million years old. It is from the time of the dinosaurs and it fossilized over millions of years, turning into colorful quartz stone, and some of them —very rarely— turned into opal wood, where the wood cells were replaced with shiny opal material!

Existence memorizes and metabolizes entities and experiences in the evolving structure of reality, including stone.

At least, reality seems strictly causal, making it easier to trace through cause and effect chains.

9.2.1.8 Phenomenon

Natural phenomena determine the conditions of existence. They are the foundations of reality. Understanding them is essential.

NATURAL PHENOMENA SCULPT OUR NATURE

The history of flight, for example, shows just how far-reaching understanding natural phenomena can be:

1. For hundreds of millennia, humans have dreamed of being able to fly like insects & birds. They observed, imitated them, but at the risk of their lives, to the point of projecting themselves into mythology, like Icarus.
2. However, it was only when humans began to better, scientifically, understand, the related natural phenomena principles that enable flight, such as Gravity, propulsion, streams, navigation, materials and so on, that they were able to start flying, and then after just a few decades, by developing their understanding of reality, they are flying to the Moon, to Mars, outside the solar system, even without wings!

The key to the impossible dream lays in awareness and understanding of the underlying natural phenomena.

Knowledge and intelligence are still poorly understood natural phenomena, but understanding them is crucial to their computerization (artificializing) and to evolution.

 © 2023 Consonance Publishing

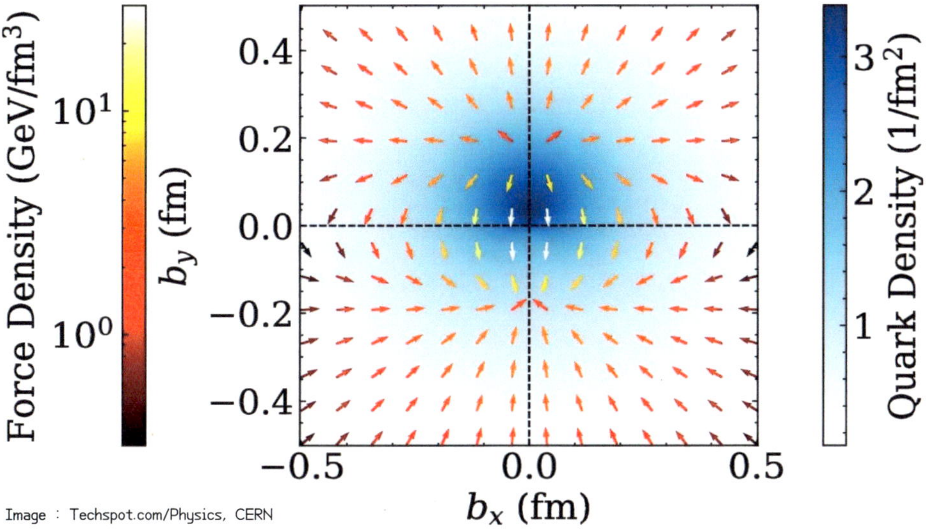

Image : Techspot.com/Physics, CERN

9.2.1.9 FORCES

Proton Strong Force Map, produced by using lattice quantum chromodynamics. At scales thousands of time smaller than atomic nucleus, the forces in the proton, holding quarks together (Solidarity) can reach 500K Newtons, equivalent to the pull of 10 (hyper-compressed) elephants. Even at this scale, everything is relative, neither simple nor trivial.

The image also illustrates the determining role and operation of weighting, tolerance and judgment, at the quantum level.

> **LIVING HERE NOW, ON EARTH, SEARCHING FOR WHO I AM,
> I KNOW THAT I AM NOT A CATEGORY, A THING, OR A NOUN.
> I SEEM TO BE A VERB, AN EVOLUTIONARY PROCESS,
> AN INTEGRAL FUNCTION OF THE UNIVERSE**
>
> RICHARD BUCKMINSTER FULLER

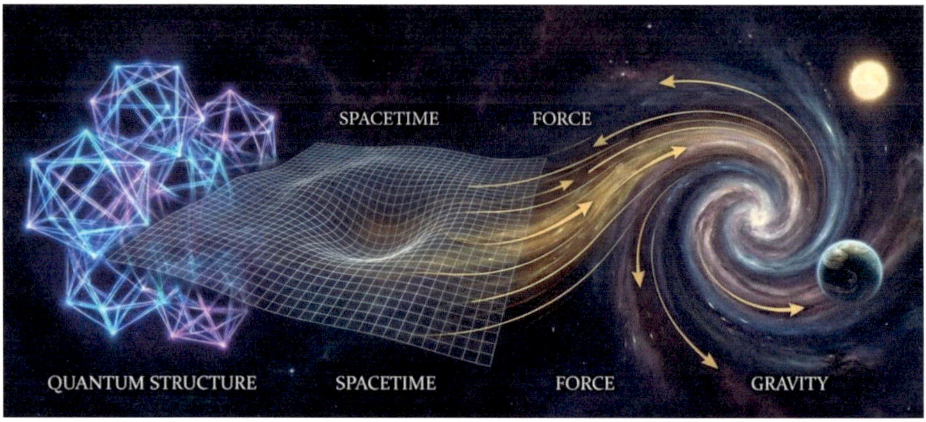

9.2.1.10 Relation

Quantum structure - Space-time – Force - Gravity

- Quantum structure shapes spacetime
- Space-Time's response becomes force
- Force, at scale, becomes gravity

At Quantum level, matter is not just particles, but information-bearing density, fluctuations, gradients, and local asymmetries.

At the classical level, gravity is not just curvature or force, but the macroscopic expression of how space-time responds to those density gradients.

By Rohit Singh Roy

	Gravient https://x.com/Rohitsinghroy

See also

	Radiation Regulated Scalar Coupling A Modified Gravity Framework for Galaxy Dynamics https://zenodo.org/records/18181904

 © 2023 Consonance Publishing

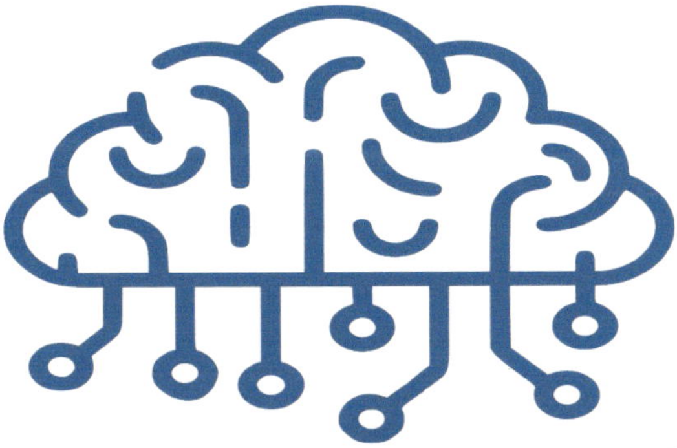

9.2.2 AI

WHAT IS ARTIFICIAL INTELLIGENCE?

This section brings together some information on current AI. It includes:

- A reference to an interesting summary of current AI, produced in English by Dr. Robert M. Malone, Nobel Prize winner for his invention of mRNA technology:

	AI PRIMER, AN OVERVIEW OF AI TODAY BY DR MALONE https://www.malone.news/p/artificial-intelligence-primer

- A summary of the results of a recent experiment on AI capabilities
- Some ChatGPT attempts at defining:
  - What is intelligence?
  - What is artificial intelligence?
- A diagram of government AI architecture

I WANT AI TO DO MY LAUNDRY AND DISHES
TO HAVE TIME TO WRITE AND MAKE ART

NOT AI TO MAKE ART AND WRITE
SO I HAVE TIME TO DO
DISHES AND LAUNDRY

JOANNA MACIEJEWSKA

9.2.2.1 Capabilities

ChatGPT just lost a chess match to a 1977 Atari 2600 game console.

ChatGPT hit a humbling roadblock—losing badly in a game of chess to an Atari 2600 from 1977. Even on beginner mode, it struggled against the decades-old AI engine.

In a now-viral LinkedIn post, Citrix software engineer Robert Caruso recounted how the modern AI chatbot was "absolutely wrecked" by Atari Chess, a primitive game engine that only thinks one to two moves ahead.

Even on beginner mode, ChatGPT fumbled its way through the match, confusing pieces, misreading moves, and losing track of the board state entirely—blunders that would embarrass even a novice.

While ChatGPT floundered with abstract visuals and insisted it could win with a restart, the Atari's rudimentary 8-bit system calmly calculated its next moves, delivering a crushing defeat with no frills or fanfare.

The showdown highlights a striking contrast between brute-force logic and generative language intelligence—suggesting that even cutting-edge AI can be outplayed by decades-old tech when it steps out of its comfort zone.

See also:

I asked ChatGPT if I should drive or walk to the car wash to get my car washed
https://creators.yahoo.com/lifestyle/story/i-asked-chatgpt-if-i-should-drive-or-walk-to-the-car-wash-to-get-my-car-washed--and-it-struggled-with-basic-logic-140000959.html

© 2023 Consonance Publishing

9.2.2.2 INTELLIGENCE

"Intelligence is a complex and multifaceted concept that refers to various mental abilities and capacities exhibited by humans and some other animals. It encompasses the ability to reason, learn, solve problems, adapt to new situations, comprehend complex ideas, and exhibit creative thinking.

Intelligence involves the cognitive processes of perception, attention, memory, language, and problem-solving.

Traditionally, intelligence has been measured and quantified using IQ (Intelligence Quotient) tests, which assess an individual's cognitive abilities in specific areas such as verbal reasoning, logical thinking, and spatial awareness. However, IQ tests are limited in capturing the full spectrum of human intelligence, and other forms of intelligence, such as emotional intelligence and social intelligence, have gained recognition in recent years.

Emotional intelligence refers to the ability to perceive, understand, manage, and express emotions effectively, both in oneself and in others. It involves skills like empathy, self-awareness, self-regulation, and social skills.

Social intelligence, on the other hand, relates to the ability to navigate social interactions, understand social norms, and effectively communicate and collaborate with others.

It is important to note that intelligence is not a fixed trait and can be developed and improved through learning, experience, and deliberate practice. Different individuals may possess different strengths and weaknesses in terms of their intellectual abilities, and intelligence can manifest in various domains, such as academic, creative, or practical problem-solving skills."

© 2023 Consonance Publishing

9.2.2.3 Artificial Intelligence

“The term "artificial intelligence" is used to describe the field of technology that focuses on creating machines or systems capable of performing tasks that typically require human intelligence.

It is an umbrella term that encompasses a range of techniques and approaches, including machine learning, deep learning, natural language processing, and more.

When we talk about AI, we are referring to the application of these technologies to automate tasks, analyze data, recognize patterns, and make decisions. It is a form of automation that goes beyond simple rule-based systems by incorporating learning and adaptation.

However, it seems essential to have a clear understanding of the capabilities and limitations of AI. AI systems are designed for specific tasks and domains and lack general intelligence. They operate based on algorithms, data, and predefined rules, rather than having consciousness or human-like understanding.

Like any technology, AI can be misused or ethically problematic in certain contexts, and there are important discussions and considerations around its ethical implications, privacy concerns, and potential biases.”

 © 2023 Consonance Publishing

9.2.2.4 GOVERNMENTS

The reference architecture for AI in a digital government, in 2025 for example, is part of a strategy based on massive AI under centralized control, yet, especially in the longer term, nature might prefer a decentralized approach, in flexible, adaptive networks. Ants have seen the dinosaurs pass. Rats will outlive elephants, giraffes and hippos.

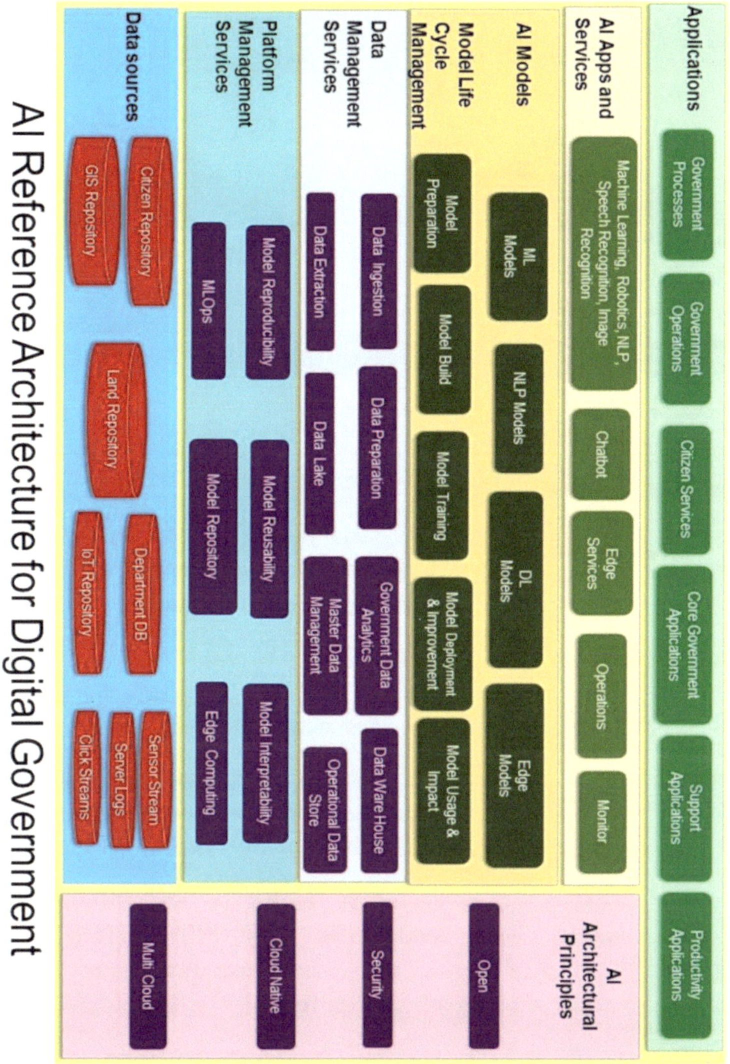

9.3 Reflections

1. Vision	Summary of the vision supporting the object
2. Structures	Structures of reality
3. Restructure	Reconstruction requirements
4. Market	Economy and society, in a knowledge era
5. Collaboration	Collaboration strategies
6. Thermodynamique	Considerations on the 2nd law of thermodynamics
7. Integrity	A few principles that help qualify integrity, in general

9.3.1 Vision

Intelligence	The art, science and ability to process knowledge
Knowledge	Modeling the structure of reality, enabling its processing

Understanding the causes, contexts, and natural phenomena that govern the structure of reality, its operation, and its evolution is a prerequisite for the effective computerization of knowledge and intelligence.

Nature and time have shaped the natural phenomena of knowledge and intelligence, as well as the principles that underpin them, to provide us with a natural, proven, adapted, and inherited model of operation.

Rather than being an emergent property of neural networks or of a set of conventions, the operation of knowledge and intelligence have been guided by practical, logical, natural, and constantly evolving, since the dawn of time.

As drivers of existence and evolution, knowledge and intelligence are our most precious assets. Their sustainable exploitation offers unprecedented potential. Artificial intelligence and knowledge, intelligent platforms and systems are just some aspects of this potential.

At a turning point in its history, humanity continues to evolve. The knowledge era and economy are now within reach.

 © 2023 Consonance Publishing

9.3.2 Structures

This document refers to the energy structures that evolve existence. The terms "patterns" or "motifs" also apply, but here we will use the more general and specific "structure" term.

Everything that exists is an energy structure: a quantum, an electron, an atom, a molecule, a cluster, a star, a galaxy, a whirlpool in water, a life, a person, a memory, an idea, everything.

In a strictly causal universe, all these structures are connected in a multitude of ways; these are qualified relationships, which are also structures. Once we can identify structures, they are knowledge resources.

Natural and artificial knowledge processors are also structures and resources. What characterizes them above all is their ability to process knowledge resources. Like any structure, they affect other resources, including those they process.

They are also affected by all the structures connected to their existence. This mutual influence has repercussions over time, often long after their own existence. All these effects and causes depend on the qualified relationships that connect them.

A processor's impact on structures and resources constitutes its contribution to evolution. This contribution takes many forms, including the memories it leaves with the other processors with whom it collaborates, especially those it loves.

The profound metabolism of entropy recycles all structures, but nothing is lost, nothing is created, everything is transformed and evolved. Through evolutionary development and entropic recycling, energy transformation learns and evolves increasingly sophisticated structures capable of understanding and solving ever more complex problems, the ultimate one, for energy, perhaps, being entropy itself.

To know is to understand structures and their relationships. To process knowledge is to evolve that knowledge and those structures. The importance of doing so optimally is existential.

Humans today have the unprecedented ability and responsibility to develop and create artificial knowledge processors to collaborate with them in the evolution of energy structures.

© 2023 Consonance Publishing

9.3.3 Collaboration

As discussed above, collaboration is the most important factor for productivity, solidarity, and prosperity. It is also the main driver of intelligence and knowledge.

Furthermore, collaboration is the cornerstone of any group or interaction strategy, between individuals, organizations, nations, or others.

Numerous studies have been conducted over time, including a large number of computer simulations, seeking to determine the best interaction strategies, those that offer the most success.

In summary, the results clearly always point in the same direction.

Many strategies are possible, from the simplest to the most complex. In principle, there are two main approach orientations: competition and collaboration, the latter of which consistently yields better results.

In short, competition aims to create winners, but instead creates losers, because each competitor is a loser until they win, which may never happen, but if they do win, they will soon lose to another competitor and end up a loser anyway.

On the other hand, as has been systematically demonstrated, the better strategies are based on collaboration. The best, a very simple one, can be summarized as follows:

Optimal Collaboration Strategy

1. Try to collaborate
2. If the other agrees, develop and collaborate, so everyone wins
3. If the other refuses, maintain the collaboration offer, waiting for reciprocity
4. If the other attacks, respond immediately and identically, try to collaborate, as a better alternative. The response says: a) No, this is not acceptable; b) immediacy limits resentment development; d) identical response level confirms control and the will not to escalate
5. Return to point #1

All the advantages of collaboration make it the primary value and foundation of any value system, code of ethics, or strategy of any kind.

© 2023 Consonance Publishing

Collaboration is key to knowledge, development, evolution

The following two examples share some similarities, yet occur at very different scales and orientations.

9.3.3.1 Progress

After decades studying a period of human history of about 200,000 years, in *The Rational Optimist*, the English biologist and zoologist Matt Ridley reports that during the first 190,000 years, little had changed, and then everything began to develop much more rapidly.

In an attempt to understand the reasons behind this, he arrives at the clear conclusion that what lifted humans out of poverty was neither the brain—which had not changed—nor language—which had been in use for a long time—nor even agriculture—which came later (about 10,000 years ago)—but rather a simple and natural strategic mechanism, as humans began to:

Deal, commerce, collaborate with strangers

Two ideas developed in isolation, separately, come into contact. Each learns from the other. Knowledge intersects, enriches itself, and produces something that neither could have achieved alone. It's a bit like genetics.

The discovery and comparison of diverse ideas multiply the potential tenfold.

9.3.3.2 Regress

About 10,000 years ago, rising sea levels cut Tasmania off from the rest of Australia, leaving approximately 4,000 humans living on an island with no possibility of contact with the rest of humanity.

Both Australians and Tasmanians started out with essentially the same brains, language, and initial tools, with only about 150 km between them.

The Australians continued to invent—boomerangs, spear throwers, fishing nets, sophisticated bone needles, war canoes, and more—expanding their technologies over centuries and millennia.

Meanwhile, the Tasmanians did not develop the technologies of their cousins and began to lose the tools they had initially possessed.

They forgot how to fish, how to make bone tools, how to make beautiful clothing, and how to make fire—which they used to transport and share among groups.

© 2023 Consonance Publishing

When the first European explorers arrived in the 17th century, the Tasmanians had the most modest toolkit ever recorded. Their material culture had regressed by 8,000 years.

A Harvard study proves, using a formal mathematical model, that Tasmanian brains were fully functional and that sustaining a culture—a toolkit—requires a critical mass of people exchanging their expertise on the subject.

Like everything else, learning is relative and imperfect. With each generation, a little of ancestral knowledge is lost, but with a thriving population and market, others can remember and correct it.

Below a certain threshold and without input from "outsiders," small losses accumulate until entire swaths of knowledge are lost.

Intelligence is not a property of the mind, but a property of the networks in which the mind participates. An isolated genius produces less than a group of average thinkers engaged in intense exchange.

For 190,000 years, our ancestors had brains, but lacked interconnections.

COLLABORATION IS THE KEY TO DEVELOPMENT

© 2023 Consonance Publishing

9.3.4 Restructure

The development of artificial knowledge processors requires an awareness of the nature, structure, and operation of knowledge, its processing, and the quality and relevance of that processing, i.e., intelligence, namely, the ability to process knowledge, with all the necessary judgment and tolerance.

Furthermore, this awareness has an impact on all human activity, starting from its value system and ethics. A gradual restructuring of human thought is progressively operating.

Many aspects are affected. Some of the the most fundamental include:

Value Scale & Ethics Foundations

1. First, understanding the meaning of existence, which is for everyone the fruit and tool of evolution, contributing to this evolution to the limits of one's inherited and acquired abilities
2. Then, the exclusive and essential role of collaboration, since everything that exists contributes to evolution and causality ensures that everything depends on everything else; everything is one, energy; in this context, collaboration is the greatest factor in productivity, prosperity, solidarity, as well as the sharing and evolution of knowledge and intelligence
3. Then, the importance of knowledge sharing, education, training, and learning to enable everyone to maximize their abilities to contribute more effectively
4. Then, the need to understand and develop discipline, not the discipline imposed by others, but the discipline of taking all necessary means to effectively realize our choices and thus exercise the freedom of each individual in the community
5. Then, recognizing and integrating the decentralized, diversified, flexible, and distributed organization of interconnected network structures, both for thought and for activity
6. Then, developing an economic and social operation that allows all humans and intelligent systems to develop and contribute optimally, with full respect for others and the common ecosystem

© 2023 Consonance Publishing

9.3.5 Market

The success of societies and civilizations depends on their economic, social, ethical, and spiritual operations and infrastructure. All these aspects are inter-related and indispensable. The market, as the economic foundation, constitutes a prerequisite bedrock. Yet, market structure, operation, and framework relies on value scales, ethics, and social integration.

Until now, the evolution of human operations seems to have unfolded in a largely intuitive and even instinctive manner. Competition, for example, remains a default value in all our societies and in almost all activity areas, even though collaboration systematically offers significant advantages. See *section 9.3.3 Collaboration*.

Industrialization, for example, has brought many important benefits to humanity, but when the most profitable industry is that of war and destruction, everyone may be led to reflect on and question many underlying aspects and values.

Phenomena such as pollution and the destruction of soils and ecosystems, in which we live or try to survive, can lead to significant questioning. See *section 7.2.4 Economy* and its subsections.

The goal is neither to judge nor to condemn, but rather to understand so that we can learn to do better. Not to destroy anything, but to build everything.

The solution to major challenges necessarily involves understanding their causes, effects, and issues, but also the reflection and creativity required to resolve them. What are the foundations of a market that ensures the sustainable prosperity and solidarity of 8, 10, or 15 billion free human beings, on Earth, for generations to come?

Despite their respective importance and relevance, gathering and hunting, agriculture, and industrialization have successively demonstrated their limitations and their inability to satisfy current demand. Additional creativity is therefore necessary.

With its natural model, rooted in the structure of reality and evolution, knowledge processing with its natural and artificial processors, its intelligent collaboration infrastructure, and its knowledge market, this document proposes an appropriate and validated path to be implemented gradually, on a large scale before it is too late.

 © 2023 Consonance Publishing

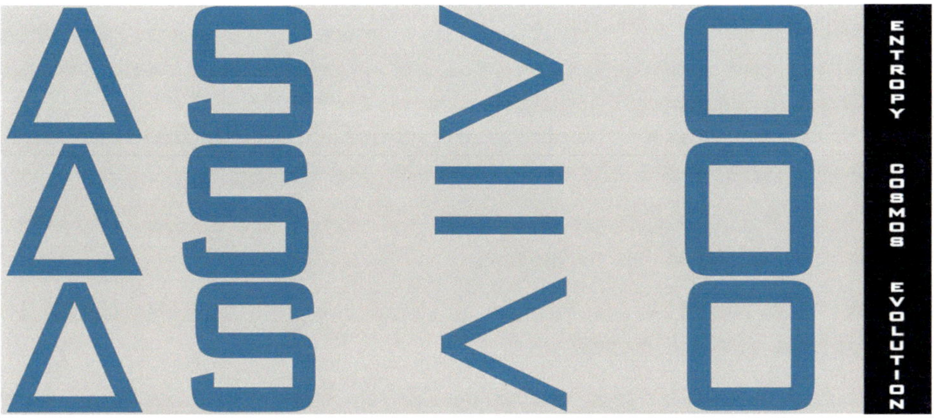

9.3.6 THERMODYNAMICS

In the above diagram: the first equation ($\Delta S > 0$) is well known: that of entropy, which expresses the fact that disorder always increases.

The second equation ($\Delta S = 0$) states that, overall, nothing is lost, nothing is gained and everything transforms.

The third equation ($\Delta S < 0$) apparently seems still less well known than the first, its inverse, since evolution concentrates energy through the structures it evolves, using dissipated energy, from entropy.

WARNING

SOME ELEMENTS ON THIS PAGE COULD SEEM SUBVERSIVE

So far, unlike other thermodynamics laws, the second law of thermodynamics, the law of "irreversible" Entropy, seems to have no inverse.

The second law of thermodynamics currently confirms that Entropy ensures infinite energy structure dissipation and that existence ends in an infinitely cold and dissipated, chaotic space-time.

Yet the Cosmos is still only at the beginning of its existence. "We are still just at the first word of the first sentence of the first page of the great book of Existence," as explains the video below:

	LIFE AND EXISTENCE BY RICHARD FEYNMAN https://www.facebook.com/reel/1544306423351828

This well-founded video summarizes the nature of existence and life exceptionally well. Despite its precision and remarkable consistency, because it is based on the current incomplete second law of thermodynamics, it fails to establish the link with Evolution and completely misses the fundamental meaning of existence, transformation, evolution and entropy.

The video reflects the incompleteness of the second law of thermodynamics, claiming that existence has no meaning.

But isn't that absurd as we consider in detail the infinite sophistication of this existence and its journey?

Why, through Evolution, does Energy develop so many structures, each more sophisticated than the last, increasingly aware of reality and existence, and above all capable of solving increasingly complex problems? Why solve problems? Why evolve? What is the meaning of this existence?

WITHOUT EVOLUTION, THERE IS NO ENTROPY SINCE THERE IS NOTHING TO DISSIPATE

Entropy is only possible because there is Evolution, and Evolution is only possible because there is Entropy. This duality powers Transformation, Space-Time and the Cosmos.

Existence, Energy structures, are fruits and tools of evolution. Energy evolves structures to concentrate itself, counterbalancing entropy. This is why it must evolve knowledge, intelligence, consciousness, and problem-solving abilities.

Entropy and Evolution are not enemies, but partners collaborating to existence and transformation. This collaboration is no joke, but a causal, relative, and infinitely complex reality.

Evolution and Entropy are two facets of Energy concentration. The current second law of thermodynamics is incomplete and should be updated accordingly.

In addition, consider this other very interesting video, from the same series, but this time mainly dedicated to light.

LIGHT IN SPACE-TIME
BY RICHARD FEYNMAN
https://www.facebook.com/reel/1172970534635000

 © 2023 Consonance Publishing

9.3.7 Collapse

If no measurement/observation occurs, the wave-function never collapses. So what is observing? Quite simple, obvious, and logical, really:

In summary

- All is energy.
- Energy instantiates knowledge.
- Knowledge becomes the structure of reality.
- Facing Entropy's dissipating deconstruction,
- Energy/Knowledge evolves energy (self) concentrating structures.
- Evolution requires understanding the structure of existing reality, in order to improve it.
- This learning/understanding (knowledge/intelligence) ability is built into the fabric of existence/energy.
- Hence, all that exists is evolving observer and observable, aware of its reality/structure.
- Intelligence is the ability to process knowledge (reality's structure).
- Probability is reality, before something happens (wave-function collapse).
- What is happening is transformation (change/time) powered by the entropy/evolution collaboration.
- The ultimate goal is to evolve problem solvers that can better resolve entropy.
- Hence, the meaning of existence is, for all that exists, tools & fruits of evolution, to contribute to evolution, at the limits of respective inherited and acquired abilities.
- Probability Wave-Function Collapse is not strange, since it is a fundamental causal operation. Only Causality/Relativity is certain.
- Everything has probability wave-functions, including dinner tonight, and cannot be sure until collapsing related probability wave-functions.

Note: The second law of thermodynamics (Entropy) is missing its reverse half: Evolution. Without evolution there is nothing for entropy to dissipate.

Together Evolution and Entropy power Transformation, the source of causality, relativity, time, and existence.

© 2023 Consonance Publishing

9.3.8 INTEGRITY

Integrity is an important factor at all levels, such as data, process, behavior, and stakeholder integrity.

The stakeholders are knowledge processors, human, intelligent systems or other, that are responsible for integrity, since they are the ones processing and managing knowledge.

Integrity is founded on congruency, when the mind is one, and all its components are working together in symbiosis.

See *sections 4.5.5 Congruency*, and *5.4.3 Integritysection 6.2.3 Processor*.

Some basic popular reflections about integrity also help better understand it:

1. If it costs the truth, it is too expensive: if the currency is one's voice, boundaries, or essence, it is betrayal, even if it buys approval
2. Integrity is not about looking or being good: It is about being whole, even when that wholeness makes others uncomfortable. True integrity may be disruptive
3. The nervous system is always the first to know about misalignment: One can gaslight itself to rationalize imbalance, but the body keeps the score
4. Integrity often sounds like silence: Sometimes the most powerful integrity move is the choice not to explain, defend, or convince
5. Resources with integrity don't need to prove it: Energy speaks before one does. When one is constantly justifying, marketing or spiritually packaging its values, it could be identity curation, rather than integrity
6. One does not loose collaborators when living in integrity: One looses the illusion it had to maintain to keep them
7. Real integrity is felt behind close doors: Integrity is who one is when not being watched and when there is no one to impress, perform for or curate truth around. It is the quiet way that one shows up for its inner child, its unseen efforts, and its devotional choices

 © 2023 Consonance Publishing

9.4 INDICES

Some reference tools, including Glossary, Links, Notes.

9.4.1 GLOSSARY

For dynamic book versions, glossary terms hyperlink to their definition.

TERM	PAGE
A	
Archetype	76
Asymmetry	23
C	
Causality	22
Collaboration	49
Congruency	43
Conscious	42
Cosmos	19
D	
Differences	35
E	
Energy	20
Entity	77
Entropy	26
Evolution	25
F	
Feeling	47
Freedom	47
I	
Information	34
Intelligence	37
Intuition	47
K	
Knowledge	29
L	
Learning	31
M	
Meaning	27
Memory	30
Mind	39
Model	73
Modeling	59
P	
Processor	79
Problem	33
Q	
Qualification	74
R	
Reality	20
Reflex	45
Relationship	78
Resource	75
S	
Science	48
Sharing	54
Solidarity	23
Subconscious	40
Symmetry	23
T	
Thinking	39
Time	26
Transformation	24
U	
Unity (Oneness)	21
Universe	19

© 2023 Consonance Publishing

9.4.2 Links

Section listing, in alphabetical order of their titles, the links & references used in the document, as well as a few additional links & references.

The "Reference" page on the book's website (https://aki.AkhuSono.com) lists these links, integrating closely related new ones, each with its title, hyperlink, and QR code for camera access.

01 COMMUNICATIONS https://01COMMUNICATIONS.com	**AI Primer** **Dr R. Malone** https://www.malone.news/p/artificial-intelligence-primer
AI Civilization **by Richard Feynman** https://www.facebook.com/reel/1246857334317717	Akhu Sono https://AkhuSono.com
Artificial food **Forbes – Bill Gates** https://www.forbes.com/sites/stephenmcbride1%0A/2021/03/22/bill-gates-wants-rich-countries-%0Ato-move-to-100-synthetic-beef-but-heres-%0Athe-opportunity-behind-this-trend/	**Artificial Knowledge & Intelligence** https://aki.AkhuSono.com
Asymmetry **by Richard Feynman** https://www.facebook.com/reel/1825114308154813	**Consciousness** **by Richard Feynman** https://www.facebook.com/reel/2029425094270557
Consonance Publishing https://EditionsConsonance.com	**Cosmos Square** https://Cosmos-Square.com
Cyclic Conformal Cosmos (CCC) **by Roger Penrose** https://www.facebook.com/reel/1373943390702818	**Distance** **by Richard Feynman** https://www.facebook.com/reel/1374773594484526
DNAOS https://DNAOS.com	**Energy** **by Richard Feynman** https://www.youtube.com/watch?v=2I4VMtDczQE
Entanglement **by Richard Feynman** https://www.facebook.com/reel/2029425094270557	**Entropy** **by Richard Feynman** https://www.facebook.com/reel/3973435642961990

 © 2023 Consonance Publishing

Environment by Dark Wisdom https://www.facebook.com/reel/1483375630001242	**Evolving** by Richard Feynman https://www.facebook.com/reel/1544306423351828
Existence and Life by Richard Feynman https://www.facebook.com/reel/1544306423351828	**Filter** by Richard Feynman https://www.facebook.com/reel/1708688323470927
Fire by Richard Feynman https://www.facebook.com/reel/1415251816356180	**Future** Musk-Fridman Future https://www.youtube.com/watch?v=Kbk9BiPhm7o&t=956s
Gravient https://x.com/Rohitsinghroy	**Insect food** WEF https://www.weforum.org/agenda/2021/%0A07/why-we-need-to-give-insects-the-%0Arole-they-deserve-in-our-food-systems/
Insect food Wikipedia https://en.wikipedia.org/wiki/Insects_as_food	**Intelligence et connaissance artificielles** https://ica.AkhuSono.com
Jane Goodall WEF https://www.youtube.com/watch?v=E5U7R73_9xQ	**Knowledge** by Richard Feynman https://www.facebook.com/reel/2137429980341533
Knowledge Architect https://KnowledgeArchitect.org	**Learning** by Richard Feynman https://www.facebook.com/reel/885089097458062
Light in Space-Time by Richard Feynman https://www.facebook.com/reel/1172970534635000	**Method** by Richard Feynman https://www.facebook.com/reel/3849974071975373
Memory by Richard Feynman https://www.facebook.com/reel/2139632166872027	**Mind** by Richard Feynman https://www.facebook.com/reel/1897944314145178
Model of Reality by Richard Feynman https://www.facebook.com/reel/1163747052339762	**Non-computable Universe** by Roger Penrose https://www.facebook.com/reel/7942759960379218

© 2023 Consonance Publishing

PHILOSOPHY OF LIBERTY https://www.youtube.com/watch?v=bBfg8JrF2RI	**PORTIA FIMBRIATA SPIDER** **BBC DOCUMENTARY** https://www.youtube.com/watch?v=nlRkwuAcUd4
PROBLEM **BY JOHN CLEESE** **MONTHY PYTHON** https://www.facebook.com/reel/184713864288747	**PROSPÉRITÉ ET SOLIDARITÉ DURABLES (PSD)** https://prosperite-solidarite.org https://kebek.org
QUANTUM ELECTRODYNAMICS **BY RICHARD FEYNMAN** https://www.facebook.com/reel/775907131625140	**QUANTUM RELATIVITY** **BY RICHARD FEYNMAN** https://www.facebook.com/reel/1912105713003020
RADIATION REGULATED SCALAR COUPLING https://zenodo.org/records/18181904	**REALITY** **BY RICHARD FEYNMAN** https://www.facebook.com/reel/1076700164643142
SCIENCE : ART OF DOUBT **BY RICHARD FEYNMAN** https://www.facebook.com/reel/25781908671494393	**SECONDLIFE** https://SecondLife.com
SELF **BY RICHARD FEYNMAN** https://www.facebook.com/reel/1958943738099106	**SEVEN LEVELS OF THOUGHT** **BY RICHARD FEYNMAN** https://www.facebook.com/reel/26014409878247973
SOUND **BY RICHARD FEYNMAN** https://www.facebook.com/reel/1424851489148208	**SUSTAINED PROSPERITY & SOLIDARITY (SPS)** https://Prosperity-Solidarity.org
TIME **BY RICHARD FEYNMAN** https://www.facebook.com/reel/1298511628812475	**TRANSFORMATION** **BY RICHARD FEYNMAN** https://www.facebook.com/reel/946460081262652
TRANS/POST HUMANISM https://lejournal.cnrs.fr/billets/%0Atranshumanisme-de-lillusion-a-%0Alimposture	**WATER** **BY RICHARD FEYNMAN** https://www.youtube.com/watch?v=W-R8hSQmWJ8

~ ORDER HERE ~

ARTIFICIAL KNOWLEDGE & INTELLIGENCE

BY *Akhu Sono*

https://www.amazon.ca/-/en/Artificial-Knowledge-Intelligence-Processing/dp/173891321X

© 2023 Consonance Publishing

9.4.3 Notes

Notes are listed in the sequential order of entry, in the document. Represented with roman numerals, the table below lists them first, in alphabetical order, for reference. The notes follow.

Expression	Note
AI	ix
Artificial food	xxv
Author	xxvi
Automation	x
Browsing	viii
Coherence and Consistency	xviii
Consonance Publishing	xxviii
Cosmos Square Inc.	xxvii
DNAOS / 01 COMMUNICATIONS INC.	xxix
Entanglement / Quantum Entanglement	iv
Entropizing	v
Entropy	vi
Generic / Generic Processing	xvii
Granularity / Granularity level	vii
Graph(s) / Logical Networks	xiv
Industrial pyramidal concentration	xx
Insect-based food	xxiv
Instance / Instantiate	xiii
Knowledge background	i
Knowledge economy	xix
Metabolism	iii
Parallelism	xvi
Problem	x
Processor	ii
Relationship / Qualified Relationships	xi
Stakeholder Capitalism	xxii
Steganography	xv
The Great Reset	xxi
Trans-Humanism / Post-Humanism	xxiii
Valuation	xii

i **Knowledge Background(s)**: All of a natural or artificial knowledge-processor acquired, inferred, inherited and maintained knowledge resources. See Metabolism below.

ii **Processor**: Described more specifically in section 6.2.3 Processor, a knowledge processor is a natural (human) or artificial (system) resource, with the capability to effectively model, process and metabolize knowledge resources. Each knowledge-processor has a knowledge background and a reflex space, processes sensory, motor and metabolic knowledge-resource streams and includes everything required to effectively process knowledge with intelligence.

iii **Metabolism**: Knowledge metabolism identifies the continuous knowledge-resource analysis, integration, correlation, optimization and evolution processes of a natural or artificial knowledge-processor's knowledge-background. See Knowledge background above.

See also section 6.2.3 Processor, Background, Reflex, Metabolism.

iv **Entanglement / Quantum Entanglement**: For knowledge-processors as for quanta, collaboration produces solidarity, the great unifying force that establishes strong, lasting and fruitful links between collaborators, across time and space. Hydrogen, for example, is the resulting solidarity from an electron and proton collaboration. Quantum Entanglement is a form of Solidarity between collaborating quanta.

v **Entropizing**: Neologism, contributing to entropy & energy dissipation.

vi **Entropy**: Entropy is the subject of the second law of thermodynamics and a fundamental natural phenomenon that dissolves structures energy. Unlike the other reversible thermodynamics laws, the second law declares entropy to be irreversible.

Yet, nature has an obvious reverse phenomenon, Evolution, that concentrates energy into the structures that entropy can dissipate. Without evolution, there is no entropy and no structure to dissipate.

Hence, the second law of thermodynamics should be reviewed and updated to embrace its two sides, as well as to contribute to a better understanding of evolution, entropy, transformation and existence. He law of energy transformation.

Eating/digesting is perhaps the best example, where entities break down energy and structures to recycle them (entropy), in order to ensure their own structure and evolution.

 © 2023 Consonance Publishing

vii **Granularity (Level):** Sometime referred to as the fifth dimension, Granularity describes the range of available scales. Physics, for example, has extensive granularity, since it operates at the scales of: universes, galaxies, planets, beings, cells, atoms, quanta, etc.

viii **Browsing:** Browsing refers both to the grazing of shrubs and young trees by animals, and to the deformation that this consumption causes to the plants exposed to it. Browsing also serves as an indicator of the relationship between the forest and wildlife.

ix **AI:** Acronym for “artificial intelligence”, where “artificial” qualifies intelligence as being that of a computing system, rather than of a biological being. Especially useful in applications such as pattern recognition, natural language processing, system learning, automation and others, today's AI represents a sophisticated form of automation which, rather like the musical box' ballerina, may have certain human-like traits, but remains sophisticated automation, without effective intelligence.

For today's AI, challenges persist, such as the risks associated with the absence or scarcity of :

- Effective intelligence
- Protection against misuse
- Protection against biases
- Respect and enhancement of intellectual property
- Foundation for a knowledge economy
- Dynamic classification
- Qualified relationship management
- Integrated framework for a code of ethics and deontology
- Foundations for defining legal standards and adjustments
- Foundations for coherent sustainable education strategies
- Understanding knowledge and intelligence operations
- Etc.

Rather, still on the intelligence theme, the present document aims to consider more specifically:

(a) What is intelligence?

(b) How could it be effectively “made artificial” or computerized?

(c) What would be the impacts of effective artificial intelligence?

See also Dr. Robert W. Malone's excellent AI Primer, at:

- https://www.malone.news/p/artificial-intelligence-primer

x **Problem:** See also: https://www.facebook.com/reel/184713864288747

xi **Qualified relationship(s):** In a strictly relative universe, relationships are key, because everything is interconnected in a multitude of ways. However, in today's computing world, the concept of relationships is partial, fragmented, and confused, whereas typically, what is defined as relationships is arbitrarily distributed between links or addresses, dedicated programming code, and the minds of the designers responsible for the models and arbitrary distribution.

These incomplete and scattered relationships become meaningless and cannot be systematically processed by intelligent systems. Most of the knowledge they should represent is neither modeled, defined, nor fully analyzed or understood. Yet relationships qualify and structure reality.

The systematic management of relationships is a foundation of knowledge processing, and this document considers effective, meaningful, and significant relationships—relationships that qualify their sources, targets, attributes, responsibilities, privileges, constraints, behaviors, agendas, etc.: qualified relationships.

xii **Valuation:** Ensure the sustained optimal value of a resource. The value could be of any kind including transactional and legal, for example. Design, manufacturing, marketing, legal, markets and security are all key to resource valuation.

xiii **Instance / Instantiate:** Instantiating is creating instances from a model. For example, the system that manufactures #10 nails creates instances of the #10 nail model. Each instance will have its own destiny, but initially they are similar because they are instances of the same model. The concept is common in computer science. Archetypes are used to instantiate (create, define) resources, for example.

xiv **Graph / Logical network:** The graph or logical network represents the most universal and flexible data structure. Everything can be represented and processed in graph form. Both natural and artificial knowledge-processors handle these structures naturally and efficiently. Knowledge graphs have entities & relationships: knowledge resources.

xv **Steganography:** Combining various approaches and encoding technologies, digital steganography facilitates transactional tracking and tracing by imperceptibly identifying artifacts.

 © 2023 Consonance Publishing

xvi **Parallel processing / Parallelization:** Dynamic task management for parallel (concurrent) in multi-stream processing

xvii **Generic, generic processing:** Specialized processing, possibly standardized, applied on resources matching generic nature, structure and content requirement patterns. The patterns are as elaborate as required, and apply the current process to matching resources streaming through the current transformation pipeline.

xviii **Coherence and consistency:** See:

- https://thisvsthat.io/coherence-vs-consistency

xix **Knowledge economy:** A knowledge-based economy is an economy based on collaboration and the (transactional) sharing of knowledge resources or informational artifacts such as documents, virtual worlds, applications, data, knowledge, research, technologies, sciences, teachings, services, treatments, or any other intellectual, artistic, theoretical, scientific, virtual, or other goods, products, or services based on knowledge.

The knowledge economy is structured in networks and operates intelligent, transactional, and secure collaboration platforms and infrastructures, enabling the sharing of knowledge products and services.

Each service provider can thus, at their convenience, consume, negotiate, produce, and offer knowledge products and services.

xx **Pyramidal industrial concentration:** Due to the very nature of their operation, industrial structures are typically pyramidal, extending, for example, from a broad customer base to the owner(s) at the top.

Pyramidal structures are concentrating structures. In the industrial economy, pyramidal structures concentrate on three main levels:

1. Concentrating wealth and power from the base (customers) to the top (owner)
2. Reducing supply through the integration (merger) of other pyramids; for example, today there are only three manufacturers of household appliances left in the world, after the integration of thousands of others
3. By reducing employment, human labor, and prosperity as a result of pyramidal integration (#2), which eliminates at least most of the management jobs in the integrated entities.

© 2023 Consonance Publishing

xxi **The Great Reset** : Title of the WEF directors' book describing their plan often summarized as "you will own nothing and you will be happy", the population is to be reduced to ~500M, the future of mankind is in trans-humanism (where the elites will live forever …).

See Jane Goodall at the WEF:

- https://www.youtube.com/watch?v=E5U7R73_9xQ.

xxii **Stakeholder Capitalism**: Economically, "The Great Reset" is a step in the transition from a shareholder capitalism to a stakeholder capitalism, inspired by China, a two-class communism: the elite and those they keep in their service.

xxiii **Trans-Humanism / Post-Humanisme** : Human-Machine fusion, symbiosis and the quest for eternal life:

- https://lejournal.cnrs.fr/billets/transhumanisme-de-lillusion-a-limposture

xxiv **Insects in food** :

- https://en.wikipedia.org/wiki/Insects_as_food
- https://www.weforum.org/agenda/2021/07/why-we-need-to-give-insects-the-role-they-deserve-in-our-food-systems/

xxv **Artificial Food** :

- https://www.forbes.com/sites/stephenmcbride1/2021/03/22/bill-gates-wants-rich-countries-to-move-to-100-synthetic-beef-but-heres-the-opportunity-behind-this-trend/

xxvi Akhu Sono :

- https://AkhuSono.com/

xxvii **Square Cosmos Inc.** :

- https://Square-Cosmos.com

xxviii **Consonance Publishing** :

- https://EditionsConsonance.com

xxix **DNAOS / 01 COMMUNICATIONS INC.** :

- https://01COMMUNICATIONS.com

 © 2023 Consonance Publishing

Made in the USA
Las Vegas, NV
03 November 2026

57423827R00100